KNOTCRAFT

The Practical and Entertaining Art of Tying Knots

Allan and Paulette Macfarlan

Illustrated by Paulette Macfarlan

Dover Publications, Inc.
New York

This Dover edition
is dedicated
to the memory of
Allan Macfarlan

Copyright © 1967 by Allan Macfarlan and Paulette Jumeau Macfarlan.
All rights reserved under Pan American and International Copyright Conventions.

Published in Canada by General Publishing Company, Ltd., 30 Lesmill Road,
Don Mills, Toronto, Ontario.
Published in the United Kingdom by Constable and Company, Ltd., 10 Orange
Street, London WC2H 7EG.

This Dover edition, first published in 1983, is an unabridged and corrected re-
publication of the edition published by Bonanza Books, a division of Crown Publishers,
Inc., in 1967, under the title *Knotcraft: The Art of Knot Tying.*

Manufactured in the United States of America
Dover Publications, Inc., 180 Varick Street, New York, N.Y. 10014

Library of Congress Cataloging in Publication Data
Macfarlan, Allan A.
  Knotcraft, the practical and entertaining art of tying knots.

  Previously published: Knotcraft, the art of knot tying. New York : Association
Press, 1967.
  Includes index.
  1. Knots and splices. I. Macfarlan, Paulette Jumeau. II. Title. III. Title: Knot
craft, the practical and entertaining art of tying knots.
VM533.M32 1983   623.88'82   83-5318
ISBN 0-486-24515-2

Introduction

Not so long ago knot tying was considered by many to be an art for seamen, seasoned outdoorsmen, and specialists; but the recent rush to the outdoors, which has caught up millions of people and set them afloat and afield, has brought knot tying by amateurs into the home, aboard ship, into camp, and into other fields where they have proved equally essential.

Housewives, who formerly struggled with the formation of a granny knot, now find themselves faced with the task of tying a bowline or making a diagonal lashing in a hurry, often under adverse conditions. Teenagers, who had learned to tie some of the simpler knots and bends, now struggle with far more intricate ties, which are needed on board the family cruiser, in camp, or on the trail. Businessmen, who tackled only knotty business problems, are now studying marlinspike seamanship, because of the present trend seaward. *Knotcraft* has been written and illustrated to meet their needs for a comprehensive book on knots that not only is clearly illustrated but that also explains in simplified, practical detail how to tie many useful knots correctly in the easiest possible way.

Some books dealing with knots have sidestepped, not without reason, the difficult task of trying to explain precisely, in words, just how knots are tied and have relied on illustrations to instruct those who would learn knotcraft. The writers of this book not only illustrate how the knots may be tied but also explain in the simplest possible words just how they are tied and their purposes. It will be found advantageous to study the drawings in conjunction with the text, in order to acquire skill and speed in tying even the more complex knots, bends, and hitches.

Many novice knot tyers find the craft so fascinating that they advance far beyond the basic knots of seamanship. A number of them exhibit, on the walls of their dens, many ornamental and complex knots, carefully mounted on plaques, as proof of their prowess.

Contents

KNOTCRAFT
The Practical and Entertaining Art of Tying Knots

Knots and Ropes Through the Ages

Knots and ropes, or substitutes for them, have always played a major role in the life of mankind. Knots have been passed down through the years as a priceless heritage, from generation to generation, to those who dwell outdoors and "go down to the sea in ships." Since man first inhabited the earth, there has always been urgent need for knots, so, throughout the ages, man has used mind and skill to invent new and better knots.

KNOTS OF PREHISTORIC TIMES

It is not difficult to believe that effective knots existed in the time of prehistoric man and that they evolved as these ancients experimented with strips of skin and sinews of animals, vines, withes, and tendrils, which formed many simple and intricate knots without the aid of and far beyond the skill of early man.

In all probability, various basic knots, such as the half hitch and the slip knot, were among the first tied by human hands. There is little doubt that the overhand knot was one of the earliest knots if not the first to be formed by man for his use. From it evolved the figure-of-eight knot, much in use by the early American and Canadian Indians to fasten, with strong green thongs, the stone head to the shaft of hammer, ax, and arrow.

Stone-Age Knots

It is known that in the latter part of the Stone Age, Neolithic man wove ropes and devised simple, basic knots. Certainly, a great number of the many knots used then had reached them out of the far distant past. They also made twine, cord, and rope of woven vine tendrils, plant fibers, hair, and strips of animal skins and sinews. These improvised cords and ropes were used for many of the same purposes then as they are today, to fasten, lift, pull, or climb.

A few of these primitive knots and many improved versions of them are in daily use today; and the lives of thousands of builders, seamen, riggers, lumberjacks, climbers, outdoorsmen, and those employed in other pursuits, depend upon correctly tied, suitable knots, and strong, dependable ropes.

Ancient China

In ancient China, many knots used throughout the world today were known and used by artisans, fishermen, and outdoorsmen. The first letters of the Chinese and Japanese were knots on cords. In ancient China, a tally system of knots was in use. A similar system was also used as far away as Peru.

Ancient Egypt

It is known that the square, or reef knot, was used as a decorative device by the Egyptian jewelers over five thousand years ago.

Egyptian boatmen were adept at tying many kinds of knots, hitches, and lashings, some of which we use now in the same manner or in modified forms. Knotted ropes were used also to fasten doors in the tombs of the Pharaohs.

Rope made possible the building of the gigantic pyramids of Egypt. The Great Pyramid of Gizeh alone is 450 feet high, each side 700 feet long, and its estimated weight is nearly 5,000,000 tons. The huge stones used for the construction of the three main pyramids, of almost incredible vastness, built in an age when engineering science had hardly begun, were all hauled through desert sands and hoisted into place by human hands—and ropes!

Though ancient pictures revealed Egyptian galleys sailing on the Nile around 3000 B.C., they were far behind the times when one considers that the seamen of the island civilization that was Crete were sailing the sea in 4000 B.C. It is interesting to speculate on the sorts of knots that these early seafarers used.

The Egyptians and Phoenicians used ropes and knots skillfully for ship rigging and boat building. Some idea of the surprising skill of the Egyptians in using ropes and knots is revealed in the drawings of Egyptian ships, about 1250 B.C., showing that they were fitted with a truss consisting of a very heavy rope, supported by Y-shaped upright braces, running from near the bow to near the stern and knotted securely around the ship at these points. This brace stiffened the beam of the ship. No other such use of the truss was known until it was rediscovered in the days of modern engineering.

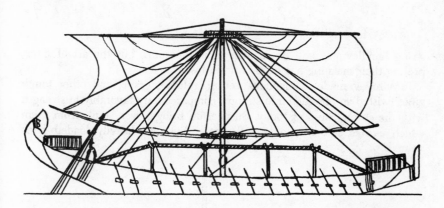

Our knowledge of knotting would be considerably richer today had the early artists and sculptors of Egypt, Greece, and Rome not been superstitious regarding certain knots. What these knots were, we shall never know, because fear that they might depict a magic knot, which would bind them for all time or enmesh them in evil spells, prevented many of these early artists from picturing knots in places where knots were certainly used. Loincloths, sails, anchors, moored galleys, and chariot harness were pictured in minute detail, but with none of the knots necessary to hold these objects in place. A fold in cloth, a short piece of rope, depicted in an artistic form or coil, concealed or replaced the knots.

Ancient Peru

About the time of the ancient Egyptians, the Incas of Peru were tying intricate knots and using knots in their tally systems. Today, some Peruvian shepherds tally their sheep by a similar method. The complex *quipus,* or knot records, of the Incas are something about which to wonder and speculate. By means of knots tied in strings and cords, combined with various colored cords, the Incas kept accurate and, for them, easily readable records embracing astronomical data, census, laws, events, and perhaps mathematical calculations, among numerous other things. These carefully guarded

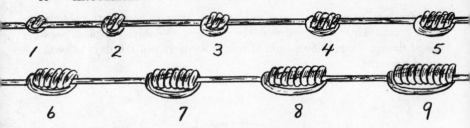

string bundles may still be seen in some museums, but the art of inter-
preting their meaning has been entirely lost.

Inca ropes, made of maguey (century plant), grape, and other tough
vines twisted and braided into strands, compared very favorably in strength
with the strong ropes of today. Suspension bridges were built from them
which carried not only men and armies but also heavily loaded pack
animals.

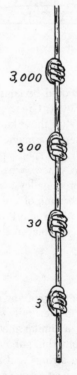

The Near East

Prior to the time of the Assyrians and the unknown date of man's greatest invention—the wheel—ropes, millions of pounds of them, did the work of the wheel.

Xerxes, mighty ruler of Persia and conqueror of the Greeks, had ten-odd miles of Phoenician and Egyptian ropes, some of them at least twenty-six inches in circumference, especially made to lash his incredible bridge of boats together. Across this bridge, spanning the Hellespont, surged his armies, bound on the victorious conquest of the Spartans and Greeks, and the occupation of Athens.

Early Greece and Rome

That the early Greeks and Romans used a number of the knots of today is evinced by examining some of their sculpture and jewelry.

The square knot, reef knot, so useful today, was tied in exactly the same way by the early Greeks and Romans. This knot generally appeared on the staff of Mercury. It was known to the Greeks as the "Knot of Hercules," who they believed had invented it. It is used today for tying bandages because it lies flat and irritates neither the wound which it covers nor the surrounding flesh. The Roman writer Pliny wrote around 60 A.D. that wounds healed much faster when the bandages used were tied with Hercules Knots.

The Romans made wire rope, unknown in the United States until the 1840's, by weaving together strands of thin copper wire.

Knots have played starring roles in ancient and not-so-ancient history, as well as legend. When the Gordian knot is mentioned, we visualize Alexander the Great struggling vainly to undo the knot which held the yoke of the cart, or plow, or chariot—legends differ—in the Temple of Zeus. King Gordius, formerly a Phrygian farmer, had tied or perhaps woven the intricate knot, which showed no ends. An oracle had proclaimed that he who undid the thick, complex knot would one day be master of all Asia. In consequence, the mysterious, master knot was worn from being handled by many strong fingers which had met defeat in their struggle with it. The fingers of Alexander also failed—but not the bite of his sword blade!

The Mayas

The wondrous temples of the civilized Mayas of Central America could never have been built without ropes to haul the gigantic blocks of stone from the quarries to use in the haulage and hoisting.

TOWARD MORE MODERN KNOTS

With the passing of the centuries, man's intelligence increased; and his growing knowledge and skill combined to invent more complex knots for carrying out more complicated tasks. Men probably devised knots such as the sheet bend (weaver's knot) and the carrick bend, using the square, or reef, knot as a basis for experimentation, then went on to form more intricate knots.

Not only have knots been devised but they have also been developed and improved to assure easier tying and greater efficiency. Not infrequently novice knot tiers have originated a simple, functional knot when trying to copy a complicated knot tied by an expert.

Europe

In the days when knights were bold, stout ropes helped to make it possible to guard the knights and their families who lived in castles. Guardians of the gates in medieval England and Northern Europe raised and lowered the drawbridges over moats by means of ropes, skillfully tied to bridge and castle wall.

From early days, in Britain and elsewhere, various guilds, such as the Builders' and Weavers', had functional knots and devoted time to developing new knots and more efficient ways of tying the ones already known to them. Sailors and fishermen also played an important part in the development of useful knots, bends, hitches, lashings, and various sorts of splices. Around 1620, Captain John Smith was intrigued by seafaring knots and learned to tie them correctly and speedily.

A number of individuals contributed useful knots during the years, and some of these knots, despite the passage of time, still retain the names of their inventors. One example is the well-known Matthew Walker knot, named after its seafarer inventor.

The Americas

Improvised ropes of various kinds were used throughout the Americas by Indian tribes long before the white invaders came. The early pioneers also had to "manufacture" rope, frequently from sources provided by Nature. A little later, pioneer women wove flax fiber on their spinning wheels into strong linen threads and also made twisted tow into crude but useful "rope."

Outdoorsmen, including the gauchos of the pampas, and the cowboys of the plains, used rope daily; and the early sailing ships required rope then as they have throughout the centuries. About fourteen years after the Pilgrims landed, rope walks for the commercial manufacture of hemp rope were established in Salem, Massachusetts, and elsewhere in America. The ever-increasing need of rope for the ships being built, as well as the demands of the colonists, caused many rope walks to be set up, in the fields in many cases, throughout New England and along the Atlantic Coast.

Rope making soon became a major industry; rope could hardly be turned out fast enough to meet the enormous demands of war and peace. The new canal systems required much rope so that the barges could be towed by horses pulling on sixty-foot lengths of it. When the railroads arrived, men could neither keep up with the demand for ropes of all sorts nor supply ropes strong enough to build the suspension bridges needed for traffic across wide rivers, or even the narrow ones, which barred the way of the iron horse.

Though copper ropes had been used effectively in the days of the Romans, wire rope was unknown commercially in America until a young immigrant from Germany, John Roebling, started making rope from strands of iron wire. Soon, great factories were turning out hundreds of thousands of miles of wire ropes of different sorts, not only for use in building bridges but also for many other purposes, such as hoists and "vertical railways," now known as elevators.

Despite great changes wrought by the coming of the Space Age, the demand for rope of all kinds increases daily, and this demand is incredible. One trend, in the time when space will be disfigured by countless space platforms and by formerly earthbound people strolling in space, will be toward special thin, lightweight and featherweight ropes, of incredible strength, now in experimental stages.

Doubtless, specially processed nylon and polyethylene will not lose favor, and it is quite possible that in the foreseeable future, one-time earthlings, living in Sirius, will be walking their Airedales and Skye Terriers around the constellations of Canis Major, in harnesses and leashes made of sky-high nylon.

KNOT MAGIC

In very early days, among primitive people throughout the world, knots of various kinds have been linked to supernatural powers and magic, often black. Three knots were often tied in cords to assure the working of strong magic; naturally, nine knots on a cord were considered even more potent. Such knots, in order to be truly effective, were supposed to be tied by those who practiced the magic arts.

Chaldea

Chaldean magic knots, originating in ancient Chaldea, region of astrology, mysticism, and magic, were considered of great potency until the Middle Ages.

Greece

Plato wrote recommending death as a fitting punishment for those who injured others by means of magic knots.

Mexico

When treating a sick person, Aztec priests consulted fate by throwing a bunch of short cords, tied together, onto the ground. If the cords bunched together, the patient would die, it was believed, but if the cords opened out, he would live. Later, Mexican priests cast lots with short lengths of cord knotted together. Mexican wizards thought they could stop the advance of Cortes by tying magic cords interlaced with paper strips to trees in a pine forest.

Europe

Witches in England claimed the power to tie up the winds in knots, each of varying force, tying three "wind knots" on short lengths of cord. Gullible seafaring men and others who firmly believed in witchcraft eagerly bought these knot strands in the hope of using them if becalmed or for other, more shady purposes. These "magic wind knots" were also sold by sorcerers in Lapland, Finland, and Greenland, and they found as much favor there as in many other parts of the world.

Various peoples in Europe believed, in early times, that the use of certain knots could cause or cure various illnesses. Their beliefs were supported by law, to the extent that many persons were executed for having bewitched others by using magic knots.

Lover's Knots

According to the beliefs of ancient sorcerers and people in general, the world around, knots had great magic powers, especially in love. Lover's knots of many different sorts were often symbols of love and a tie between lovers, but other love knots could also be used to counteract love and inspire hate.

Lover's knots, tied and woven and used as pledges in early Britain, continued through the medieval period and long after. English literature and ballads of the sixteenth century often dealt with the subject of lover's knots, especially a "true lover's knot." Despite these facts, nothing has been passed down through the centuries to help identify this knot, nor can it be classified as any particular, known knot of today. Knots depicted on old illuminated parchments and books of English origin that date through the fourteenth, fifteenth, and sixteenth centuries and beyond depict various lover's knots, but none of them claims to be *the* true lover's knot.

AMERICAN INDIAN ROPE AND KNOT CRAFTSMEN

The early American Indians tied many clever knots to serve different purposes and used varied lashings and hitches to hold things in place, such things as dog and horse harnesses, tepee and travois poles, travois bundles, packs on the backs of horses, and points on arrows and lances. The major advantage of these Indian knots and lashings was that they held. So often life was dependent on the knot's being sure and secure that few if any Indians ever tied a granny knot. Indian knots had to meet three major tests successfully: to be tied quickly and with comparative ease; to serve effectively the purpose for which they were intended; and to remain tightly knotted despite pull and strain.

The factor of knots' being easy to untie was not one of great importance to the Indians because they had an abundance of rawhide thongs for knotting and lashing—and a keen knife was always handy to sever them when they had served their purpose. Another reason why Indian knots were usually very hard to undo was that they were tied with green rawhide thongs or wet buckskin strips, both of which set like iron when dry.

Indians were able to tie knots quickly and under unfavorable conditions, such as in darkness, under water, when running, and while galloping on horseback.

Indian Rope Makers

Many Indian tribes throughout America were skillful rope makers. The habitat of the tribes helped to decide the sort of ropes they made. Nearly all the tribes of the Northwest Coast, the Southwest, the Plains, the Northeast, and the Southeast used special materials and techniques in rope making. For instance, among the cord- and rope-making materials used by the Haida and the Nootka, of Vancouver Island, who were mighty hunters of whales, were whale sinews twisted into rope of various thicknesses. The magnificent red cedars of their islands provided small limbs, fiber, and bark for the making of twisted ropes.

Many tribes of North American Indians made cords and rope from the second layer of bark of the basswood tree. This was their favorite rope-making material, but they also used the inner bark (the outer bark being too rough, in most cases) of elm, hickory, and red cedar, chiefly, and hemp, nettle stalks, and the roots of cottonwood, hemlock, and pine. The Indians of the Southwest also used horsehair and the hairs from horses' tails in making ropes, while the tribes which had no horses used the hides of various animals and animal sinews for the same purpose. Buffalo, moose, elk, and deer hides were cut into strips and these were further reduced in size and thickness until the Indians had rope, thongs, and cord which they put to many uses. These Indians frequently braided their ropes instead of twisting them. Many of the Indians were real craftsmen in the art of rope making. The women of the tribes often did their share of rope making, and some were as skillful as the men at that craft.

Most Indians tied knots skillfully and spliced and wove lines of various sorts for making fishing lines, fish nets, and trapping nets, and in joining ropes. Many tribes also used knotted cords for recording dates and marking the passage of time.

Some Indian tribes of North America and Canada used thongs and knots in the making of toboggans, snowshoes, and the net for lacrosse sticks.

The Seri Indians of Costa Rica regarded cord very highly and used it in making colorful belts, headdresses, and necklaces. They used, among other things, fiber from the roots of mesquite, and the stalks of the agave and human hair, the latter being made into the most highly prized cordage. Their cords, of varying thickness, were sized, worked, and twisted between the fingers and then rolled with the palms of the hands on the thighs.

MAGIC KNOTS OF THE INDIANS

Like most peoples throughout the world, the American Indians believed that many knots held magic and had the power to work good and bad spells. They had good fortune knots, knots to loose and bring fair and foul weather, and web knots to tangle the feet of their enemies—by thought transference.

Cat's Cradle, known to some Indian tribes as "Web Weaving," has come down to us after having amused millions of children and grown-ups all over the world for many thousands of years. Web-weaving magic and games probably reached the American Indians and the Eskimos by way of the Orient, hundreds of years before the white men settled in their territory. The grown-ups, both men and women, firmly believed that there was mighty magic in web weaving and that spirits sometimes came to admire or deride the artistic and often very intricate designs which were formed under swiftly flying fingers. At times, Indians believed that they had been challenged to a contest of speed by a visiting Spirit and they would work with frenzied haste to finish an involved pattern before the Spirit Person challenger. Sometimes winning brought good fortune—but not always!

The Navaho say that their forefathers were taught web weaving by the Spider People, and the Zuni declare that the art of web weaving was given to them by Grandmother Spider.

The tribes of some entire Indian nations engaged in web weaving, the Algonquin, for instance, were fond of the pastime as were the Teton Dakota, who called it "the Game-of-String-Wrapped-In-and-Out-Among-the-Fingers." To mention the many tribes throughout the Americas who were addicts of Cat's Cradle would fill many pages. To mention a few of the more important groups who were adepts, the Algonquin, the Apache, the Navaho, most other tribes of the Southwest, and the Indians of the Northwest Coast can be cited.

When Indians played at web weaving, or formed intricate designs, they worked the *patterns for partners* alone, using toes, teeth, lips, and stone weights, as well as fingers, to hold the string in place. These weavers considered the steps taken in making the figures as only a means to an end, the finished design.

Cat's Cradle was called by hundreds of names by the many tribes which indulged in it. Among the names were *ma-mal-lac-bi-to*, by the Hopi, and *kokominnaoowishiyan*, by a tribe in the New Mexico territory. Perhaps we had better just call the game Cat's Cradle!

Rope Magic and Illusion

The medicine men and shamans of many American Indian tribes used ropes and cords in a great number of their feats of magic and illusion. Some Indian sorcerers could not be tied with ropes or cords so that they remained prisoners for more than a few seconds. Some escaped from many ropes which bound their hands, arms, legs, and feet, by working the release while a blanket was held in front of them for a minute or two; others simply writhed out of their complex bonds before the eyes of the amazed onlookers. Medicine men would snatch lengths of rope from the air, pull long lengths of rope from apparently empty medicine bags, and on special occasions, turn a length of rope into a snake, which would glide away at the end of the illusion.

The Makah knot tyers used to do many of the modern "decapitation" and similar tricks by the use of "false" knots.

The Maya knot tricksters demonstrated "splicing a cord in the mouth," by using a cord which to all appearances had been cut but actually was not.

Memory-Aid Knots

In days gone by, the Apache Indian Scouts, attached to the United States Army, kept track of the days of the week by tying seven knots on a string, as illustrated, the big knot, among the six smaller knots, repre-

senting Sunday. Despite this, the great majority of the medicine cords of the Southwest Indians were not regarded by their owners as possessing any mnemonic value.

Memory-aid knots account for the success of the revolt of the Pueblo Indians of the Southwest against the conquering conquistadors, which was set for the new moon in August, 1680. The chiefs of the tribes along the Rio Grande were each given a string of knots tied in a piece of yucca string. Each chief had strict orders to untie one knot each day and prepare for the uprising on the morning that the last knot was untied. The revolt was so successful that by October of that year every Spaniard had either been killed or driven out of New Mexico.

Some of the Indian tribes, especially those of the Five Nations, of the Iroquois, carried knotted "message" strands of wampum. Some of the knots formed an actual message, while others only served as memory-aids in order that the runner might deliver a lengthy message accurately, partly by reading the wampum bead-shell message and partly by repeating the verbal message which he had been given before setting out.

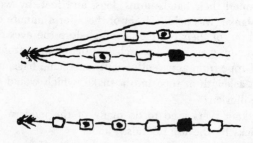

Medicine-Magic Knots

Medicine men of many Indian tribes believed in the potency of their often-complex medicine knots, used for the purposes of magic and healing. Some of these workers of magic were intricately knotted medicine cords which, they believed, served as protection against injury and sickness. In some cases, these knots appeared to be mere shapeless bundles of involved, interwoven cord, while in others, a certain amount of symmetry and attractiveness was to be found. The one illustrated here, probably a magic knot of Huron origin, is of this sort. Like practically all these mystic knots of the Indians, it has no visible beginning or ending. They were generally woven or intricately spliced, so that they could neither be undone by fingers or knife point nor correctly copied.

Many of the Apaches wore a blue medicine cord around the neck. This cord, conjured by a medicine man, was called an *izee-kloth* and was worn as a protection from harm of various sorts. Many of these cords were knotted, the number of knots ranging from three to nine, the one shown in the drawing having three knots of peculiar medicine power. Each Apache medicine necklace was made of two, three, or four cords; the most highly prized were made from antelope thongs, but buckskin and other skins were also used. The four-strand cords were regarded as especially effective in working charms or assuring protection from countless evils. Each strand of these *izze-kloth* cords was dyed a different color. The colors generally used were yellow, blue, white, and black, and many of these necklaces were decorated at intervals with olivella or other shells.

It is interesting to note that the larger and longer cords of this section of Indian country were eventually copied and used as cord girdles by certain religious orders, and that custom is still followed today.

The *mystery beads*, strung on cords, of the Mandan Indians remain one of the best-guarded secrets of American Indian medicine beads. Nothing will be told regarding them in this book since the authors were sworn to secrecy on the subject.

CORDS, ROPES, AND KNOTS IN THE BIBLE

One doing research on knots, cords, and ropes of the past would naturally consider the Bible a likely source of information. A glance at an unabridged concordance of the Bible will reveal that rope appears to be mentioned only a few times, and knots not at all.

Cords

Cords are mentioned a number of times in the Bible. One reads, "They bound Samson with two *new* cords" and "they broke their bonds and cast away restraining cords"; but nobody, apparently, either tied or unfastened a knot. They "bound sacrifices with cords," and we learn that "a three-fold cord is not quickly broken." Isaiah counsels, ". . . lengthen thy cords," but offers no advice on how to do so.

Ropes

Ropes, of immense importance in biblical times, are mentioned infrequently. The Scriptures speak of a "cart rope," and of people bringing ropes to a city so that they may "draw it into a river," and of "putting ropes on their heads," as a sign of humility and submission, but in only two or three other places is rope mentioned. Rahab, of Jericho, she of the scarlet thread, let the two spies "down by a cord through the window: for her house was upon the town wall." One can easily imagine these two young men taking a hard look at the knots on the rope which was used to lower them to safety, though knots are not mentioned. Another well-known reference to rope is when Samson, in one of his attempts to foil Delilah's purpose, suggests that if he were "bound with new ropes" he would be helpless. He wasn't!

Knots

The fact that the Bible, which tells of practically everything, apparently does not once mention the word *knot* is doubly surprising because many different knots were in everyday use in biblical times. One may read of seamen taking soundings, of fishermen making and mending nets, of workers in the fields binding sheaves and tying the mouths of sacks, of bowmen with bows, and of fowlers with snares. All these varied activities compelled the tying of various knots—yet, neither knots nor knotting is even casually mentioned in the Bible. This very absence of the mention of knots in the Scriptures raises a knotty problem.

KNOTS AND ROPE IN SHAKESPEARE

It would be passing strange, in the case of William Shakespeare, a man who knew much and wrote of practically everything, including the sea, if reference to knots and rope were not found throughout his works. A memory-refreshing visit to a few of the Bard's masterpieces can be rewarding. For instance, *in*

"Two Gentlemen of Verona," one may read of ". . . twenty odd-conceived true love knots."

"The Taming of the Shrew," Shakespeare, writing of Petruchio's horse, says that its headstall ". . . hath been often burst, and new repaired with knots . . ."

"Twelfth Night," Viola, faced with a knotty problem, exclaims, "O time! thou must untangle this, not I; it is too hard a knot for me to untie!"

"Antony and Cleopatra," Agrippa, friend of Octavius Caesar, suggests a way for Antony and Caesar ". . . to knit your hearts with an unslipping knot. . . ."

"Troilus and Cressida," one reads of ". . . another knot, five-finger-tied. . . ."

"Cymbeline," Shakespeare has a character exclaim, "Come off, come off: as slippery as the Gordian knot was hard!"

"Pericles, Prince of Tyre," one reads, "Galling his kingly hands, haling rope."

"The Comedy of Errors," an exasperated character cries, "God and the ropemaker bear me witness!"

Before leaving the Shakespearean scene, we may note that a pundit, given enough rope, or none, may pun. Shakespeare, that dynamic master of linguistics, who knew a great deal about almost everything, was a poor punster. This is surprising, since the court favorites excelled in puns which were amusing and spontaneous. Shakespeare's puns were contrived, often heavy-handed, and not always apropos.

An example of this, with *Knotcraft* as the backdrop, occurs in "The Taming of the Shrew," Act 1, Scene 2, in which Grumio warns, "An he begin once, he'll rail in his rope tricks"—a play on words, "rope tricks" replacing "rhetorics."

These few quotations help to illustrate how Shakespeare wrote for the many soldiers, sailors, and adventurers in his audience, all of whom were familiar with knots and ropes.

KNOTS IN PRINT

One of the strangest things about knotcraft is the fact that practically nothing really technical was written about knots and knotting until early in the nineteenth century.

A German named Listing was perhaps the first to write, in 1847, on the subject and theory of knotting. A good deal of what he wrote was rather naïve and, certainly, elementary, but it was a start on the subject and served its purpose at that time.

Though there are many hundreds of different knots, and almost as many variations, the authors of this book have endeavored not only to picture some of the most useful knots made today, for the use of outdoorsmen in general and seafarers in particular, but also to describe how to tie them and to mention their various purposes.

Learning the Ropes

Though there are hundreds of knots and variations of knots, the outdoorsman and the seafarer of today can get along with about twenty basic, utilitarian knots and their variations. How to tie and use these knots and many others is explained and illustrated in this book.

Good knotting has made possible the saving of countless lives and the catching of countless pounds of fish, while bad knots, of the infamous "granny" variety, have lost both fish and lives.

Today, as always, the best knots are those which tie easily, hold fast, accomplish their purpose, and untie with ease.

NATURAL-FIBER ROPES

There are many ropes and cords for many specific purposes, and the choice of exactly the right sort for the work to be done is often of major importance.

Manila

Before this age of synthetic experimentation, natural, hard-fiber Manila rope, actually abaca, woven from a species of banana plant grown in the Philippines, was considered one of the best ropes made. It was yellow-beige and was manufactured in varying thicknesses. This rope is still used a good deal aboard ship and ashore. Other fibers, made from cactuslike plants, such as henequen, were also used in the manufacture of Manila rope.

Sisal

This is a whitish hard-fiber rope, made from the fiber of the large cactuslike plant agave, grown in many parts of the world. Formerly, this rope was much in use, in place of more expensive rope.

Hemp

A soft-fiber rope made from part of a plant phloem, or bast, once much in use, this is now used less and less, except for the manufacture of high-grade cords and twines. Hemp is costly to manufacture; and its price and the new synthetic ropes, which serve better, have caused hemp to lose favor.

Jute

Rope and twines are made from this plant, largely grown in India. Though jute rope and cordage are not very strong, jute fiber is popular because it is soft and has very many industrial uses.

Coir

This is lightweight, resilient rope, made from the outer husks of coconuts. It is often woven into Manila or other rope lines to make them springier.

Cotton

Rope and cord made from cotton fiber have certain disadvantages which do not interfere with its popularity. Such rope is not very strong and it is often braided instead of twisted. Braided rope cannot be spliced and its surface is usually weak. The more expensive cotton ropes are solid-braided or hollow-braided. The popularity of cotton rope arises from the fact that it is easy to handle, runs smoothly over pulleys or through blocks, and is not expensive, except in special weaves. Soft cotton rope, about ⅜ inch in diameter, is excellent for doing knotting practice and various knotting stunts and tricks, such as those given in this book.

SYNTHETIC ROPES

Though these ropes are wonderful, they are constantly being made stronger and better for many purposes. At least twenty-five synthetic fibers have been experimented with in rope manufacture and a number of them have been made into splendid multipurpose ropes. Among these synthetic fiber ropes are polyethylene, nylon, polyester, and fiber glass.

Polyethylene

These fibers, skillfully processed from petroleum, air, and, occasionally, brine, are made into excellent ropes of various sizes and colors. The special features of these ropes are that they float and are permanently colored during manufacture. The fact that these ropes float makes them useful for water skiing and for lifesaving; and their colors, bright yellow for instance, greatly add to their visibility. These ropes are waterproof, light-weight, flexible, rot-resistant, and nearly as strong as nylon.

Nylon

This rope, conjured from coal, air, and water, is a veritable king among ropes. It has a number of advantages which natural-fiber ropes lack. It is resilient, water- and rot-resistant, and twice as strong as any fiber rope of the same size. Whether used in mountain climbing or aboard ship, it will give complete satisfaction.

NOTE: Most of the synthetic substances can be made into either braided or twisted rope, and their far greater strength makes it possible to use a synthetic rope for many more purposes than a natural-fiber rope, even if the natural-fiber rope is thicker.

CHOOSING ROPE

In this Space Age, there are ropes of all kinds to meet all demands. Some proof of this is evinced by the fact that some ropes—climbing rope, for instance—are advertised to give "*maximum* elongation under strain," while other ropes are advertised, for other uses, as having "the *minimum* stretch under strain." Yes, there are ropes for all purposes. The thing is to choose the right rope for the job it has to do.

Rope should be flexible when wet; it should be sturdy and durable, easy on the hands, easy to handle; it should repel rot and have a high breaking point.

It is well to remember that two knotted ropes, joined end to end, lose about half the strength of a single length without a join. This is the reason why ends under considerable strain are often spliced rather than knotted.

Size, Strength, and Stress

It is wise to choose a rope five times as strong as the maximum load it will have to carry. (Multiply the weight of the maximum load by five to discover what the breaking point will likely be.) Though this stress ratio of 5 to 1 appears to offer a super-safe safety margin, it is accepted as standard practice. It actually means, for instance, that a rope used to lower someone down a cliff should have a breaking strength of five times his weight. A ½-inch, three-strand Manila rope weighing about 1 pound per 13 feet, has a breaking point strength of approximately 2,600 pounds, which assures a safe work load of about 520 pounds, based on this stress ratio.

The old adage about not having a boy do a man's job applies in choosing rope. One should never try to make a small rope do the work of a large rope. This rule, of course, applies only when the ropes are made of the same material—one could not judge cotton against nylon, for instance.

The measure of rope was formerly based on its circumference, but today both the circumference and the diameter of a rope are generally given. Seafarers usually speak of the size of a rope as the circumference, while those ashore use the diameter to describe the size of a rope. More technical ways of classifying rope, such as by the number of threads of yarn in its content, need not be explained in detail here.

Dealers in rope have very specific charts which give all technical details, based on the sort of rope and the material of which it is made. Of course, this substantially affects the breaking point of different sorts of rope and the stress which each type will safely bear. Rope may usually be bought by the yard, or by the pound, or in hanks of various lengths, for various purposes.

Climbing Ropes

Preference in the choice of climbing rope has changed considerably during the past few years because of the development of much greater strength in medium-diameter climbing rope. Today, the ⅜-inch-diameter, good climbing rope is as strong as ½-inch diameter used to be. The ⅜-inch diameter assures climbers of maximum safety with the minimum weight of rope. At present, 5/16-inch-diameter rope is popular for double-rope climbing.

Rope construction has also changed enormously. In some of the top-brand climbing ropes, a core of continuous filament-type-6 nylon is used, encased in a woven sheath. Parallel, untwisted strands give far greater strength to these ropes than twisted or laid ropes. These ropes resist abrasion and ultraviolet deterioration to a surprising degree. There are also fine, cheaper ropes of white nylon and of braided, colored rope on the market which perform well.

The better ropes are water-resistant, have outstanding handling characteristics, and are made in standard climbing lengths, without knots of any sort. The actual strength of good climbing rope can be judged by the fact that the strength figures are estimated with knotted rope.

CARE OF ROPE

Rope is the outdoorsman's and the seafarer's friend; it not only merits great care but will also repay that care in many ways. Good rope responds quickly to proper handling.

Good care begins with the first uncoiling of the rope. The coil should be kept flat and the rope should be uncoiled from the center by reaching down through and pulling the tag end up through to the top, to be used as the working end. Standard rope is usually right-laid, and so it should be uncoiled counterclockwise. When the amount needed has been uncoiled, the rope should be cut cleanly with a sharp knife and the ends whipped to prevent fraying.

Care should be taken that the rope does not kink while being unwound. New rope may have to be straightened before use. A short length can be fastened overhead and a light weight attached to the end until it hangs straight without the weight. Kinks should never be pulled out of a rope by brute force; they should be unwound gently, by hand. New rope functions best after being worked with the hands, when being first unwound. Long lengths of rope should never be dragged on the ground to be straightened. Some boatmen drag them slowly astern, through the water, and campers achieve the same results by dragging rope through smooth, dry grass.

Special care has to be given to all fiber rope in order to assure its good service and long life. Such rope should always be dried thoroughly before it is stored away, neatly coiled over a round wooden peg, for instance, in a dry place. When rope is wet with salt water, it is wise to rinse it well in fresh water before drying it. Rope should be kept away from sand and grit, and such harmful substances should be brushed or washed from rope which has inadvertently been exposed to them. Insofar as possible, rope should be neither kept in direct sunlight or in hot or damp places nor exposed to frost.

Naturally, too much stress on a rope will cause it to deteriorate. This can be a dangerous state because the flaws are not visible on the outside of the rope. The cover yarn may appear in good shape but the breaks are in the inside yarns, because they are the first to break. To look for broken yarns in the heart of a rope, force a fid (see definition under "Knotting and Rope Terms" in this chapter) through the center of a strand, open it, and examine it carefully.

To get the best result from ropes, avoid jerking them needlessly, since such lack of care often causes strands to snap. Ropes used outdoors should be slackened in wet or even very damp weather. Seamen coil rope of different sorts in flat coils on the deck. Standard, right-laid rope, which was originally uncoiled in a counterclockwise manner, is coiled clockwise, "with the sun," as seamen say. Those well-versed in the care of ropes will hang them away from heat and damp, coiling them in a figure-of-eight coil on a round wooden peg. Heavy ropes of large circumference can be coiled on wooden slats, raised from the floor, thus assuring proper ventilation. For average care, rope may be coiled loosely and hung on a wooden peg, while observing the above-mentioned precautions regarding a suitable place to hang the coil.

EQUIPMENT FOR KNOTTING PRACTICE

One 6-foot length of ⅜-inch soft cotton rope, and one 3-foot length of sash cord are handy to practice knot tying. The ends of the rope and cord should be whipped so that the ends will not become frayed. The rope and sash cord can be used for knots joining two pieces of rope of unequal size. Two pieces of dowel stick, each about 12 inches long and ¾ inch in diameter, are also useful for practicing knots and hitches which are made around spars.

Identifying Rope Ends

Novice knot tyers may find it easier to tie knots if they color or whip a *red* string onto the end of the rope marked A in the drawings (usually, the end is held in the *right* hand) and leave end B uncolored. This makes it easier to identify the ends when following the written instructions and the drawing of each knot. This color marking is especially useful when making the square knot and others in which both ends of a single cord are used, in practice knotting.

KNOT-TYING TERMS

Four general terms used in knot tying should be learned by the novice before he ties his first knot. The terms, marked in the diagram, are these:

Standing Part–the inactive part of the main length of cord or rope which is worked *on*, but, as a general rule, not *with*.

Loop–shown in the drawing, is one of the basic knotting turns; it can be either overhand or underhand.

Bight–the doubled part of a rope, not including the end, between the end and the standing part.

End–either end of the rope. Throughout this book the end of the rope that is worked *with* is marked A.

LOOP   END

STANDING PART   BIGHT

These terms are used afloat and ashore; they are used in the following pages to describe how to tie knots, bends, hitches, and lashings.

Three-Turns Combinations

Knotting is made easier for novice knotters when they remember that even the most complex knots are built on three simple, basic turns: bight, loop, and overhand.

Loops

Loops are used in forming many knots, such as the bowline. A bight becomes a loop the instant the sides of the bight cross. There are two sorts of loops—the overhand loop and the underhand loop, as illustrated.

The difference between the two loops should be carefully noted. It is vast, as one will quickly discover by trying to tie a bowline with an underhand loop instead of an overhand loop.

1

2

Overhand Loop: Bring the end *over* the standing part to form a loop of the desired size. (See 1 above.)

Underhand Loop: Bring the end *under* the standing part to form a loop of the desired size. (See 2 above.)

Turns

Turns and round turns are used also in knot tying. They are made as follows:

Turn: Loop the rope once around a pole or other object.

Round Turn: Loop the rope twice around the object, as illustrated in following sketch.

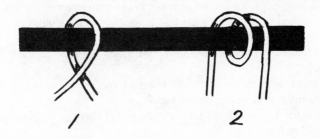

NOTE: When tying certain knots, such as the bowline, in which only one end of the rope is used, the novice should pretend that the rope is a mile long, to remind him to use only the end in hand.

KNOTTING AND ROPE TERMS

It is useful for the novice knotter to know the meaning of some basic knotting terms. With this knowledge, one or two words may be used instead of a dozen, and terse language may save lives in an emergency.

Some of the most common and useful knotting terms, used by people tied up in the world of knots, are given here. There are numerous others, connected with knotting and sailing in general, but they are either too technical or not used sufficiently to merit inclusion in this glossary.

Belay–to make a rope fast by winding it in a figure-of-eight manner around a cleat or belaying pin.

Bend–a method of binding, or making fast, two ropes together or, in sailor talk, bending ropes together, such as a sheet bend.

Bight–a loop in a rope between the end and the standing part.

Bitter end–the inboard end of a rope in use.

Cleat–a small, strong piece of wood or metal, with projecting ends, securely fastened to a fixed object. Ropes are made fast to cleats.

Clockwise–from left to right, following the direction of the hands of a clock, or sunwise, moving in the direction of the sun in its course. A term used in winding rope around a cleat or other object in this manner.

Counterclockwise–from right to left; exactly the opposite of clockwise.

Cow's tail–a frayed rope end.

Eye–a loop made, usually, at the end of a rope.

Fid–a hardwood or metal pin, which looks somewhat like a marlinspike, used for working ropes.

Grommet–an eye or ring made from rope, or metal.

Hawser–a large rope, six inches or more in circumference.

Hitch–a method of making a rope fast to another rope, a series of turns for making a rope fast to a spar or stay.

Knot–the forming of a knob in a rope by turning the rope on itself through a loop.

Lash–to bind poles or other things together by hitches or turns of rope, or to make a movable object fast.

Line–the usual nautical term for most rope and cordage in general.

Loop–see *Bight*.

Messenger–a light line used in hauling heavier rope aboard ship or onto a dock.

Mousing–a short piece of string or cord fastened across the opening of a hook, to prevent a rope from jumping out under strain.

Painter–a short length of line used to tie up small craft to a dock or mooring post.

Reeve–to pass the end of a rope through an eye, bight, or block.

Rogue's yarn–yarn of various colors woven or sewn into a rope for identification.

Rope–a term used to describe any cord over one inch in circumference.

Round turn–to pass a line completely around a spar or another rope.

Seize–to bind, with string or cord, one rope end to another piece of rope, or to bind two ropes together. There are a number of seizings, named for the work they do.

Snugged–made taut. Tightened.

Splice–to join two ropes or parts of a rope by interweaving the strands.

Standing part–the main length of rope, as distinguished from the bight and the end.

Stay–a part of a rigging used as a support for a mast.

Toggle–a small hardwood pin which is either pushed into a knot to make it more secure or more easily undone, or inserted between strands of rope for the same purpose.

Turn–a single winding of a rope around a spar or other object. A *round turn* is made by looping a rope twice around a spar.

Whip–to lash, or wind, thin cord around the end of a rope to prevent its fraying.

Knots Afloat and Ashore

The basic knots in this chapter will be found of service both afloat and ashore, as will many of the others. Apart from a number of bends, hitches, shroud knots, and special knots used for work with sails, not too many knots today can be classified as strictly seagoing knots. One reason for this is the ever-mounting popularity of cruise camping, involving tents and miscellaneous camping gear, often carried aboard the family cruiser as an integral part of cruising.

Throughout this book, knots have been arranged, insofar as possible, by categories, but the easiest way to locate any knot is to refer to the comprehensive Index. Each knot has been classified *under its own name,* which will save novice campers and seagoers the trouble of having to decide whether the tie they are looking for is a knot, hitch, or bend.

BASIC KNOTS

The overhand and the figure-of-eight knots are probably among the first basic knots discovered or devised by man. As will be seen later, these two knots are the basic knot formations of a number of others that are shown and explained in this book.

Overhand Knot

Some American Indian tribes called this "the knot that ties itself," because they had often seen it formed by nature on plant tendrils. This knot is also the beginning of the square knot, among others. It is often used as a stopper knot because, tied on the end of a rope, it will keep the rope from pulling through a hole or the small loop of another knot. It is also used at times as a temporary knot to keep the end of a small rope or cord from fraying.

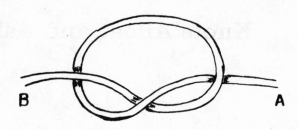

Tying. Cross end A over B and bring it around, through the loop thus formed. Pull the rope taut.

Figure-of-Eight Knot

This ancient knot, also known as the Flemish knot, is a favorite stopper knot aboard ship. It is a better one for that purpose than the overhand knot because it is bigger, much easier to untie, and less likely to jam. In addition to other stopper work, it will keep the end of a rope from running out of pulley or tackle. It is also used to make fast a rope to a cleat and as a basic formation for making certain other knots.

Tying. Make a simple underhand loop, by passing end A under the standing part, then bring end A around the standing part and up through the loop. Pull the rope taut.

STOPPER KNOTS AND HITCHES

There are literally dozens of stopper knots and stopper hitches, many of them typical seaman knots which are difficult to tie. Technically, such knots are known as end rope knots and quite a number of them are built on wall foundations and terminate in a crown knot of some sort, a number of the knots being woven or spliced as well as tied. It is because of the difficulty in tying such knots that very much easier-to-tie knots which serve the same purpose are given in this book: knots such as the stevedore's knot, the overhand knot, the figure-of-eight knot, the Capuchin knot, and the standard stopper hitch, the latter a hitch made fast to a bitt or a rail.

Standard Stopper Hitch

Among a number of stopper hitches, the standard stopper hitch is perhaps the most practical and certainly the one most in use. This knot, actually a combination of the clove hitch and an additional turn, when tied around a bitt on deck or any post, will securely hold any line even if wet or oily.

Tying. Place end A against a post, letting the standing part hang down,

bring end A around the post, then make a second turn below the first. Now, bring the end up, across the other turns, around once more, and tuck the end through, and pull taut.

Stevedore's Knot

This is a form of stopper knot used by the stevedore to prevent the fall (end) of a rope from passing through a cargo block or eyebolt.

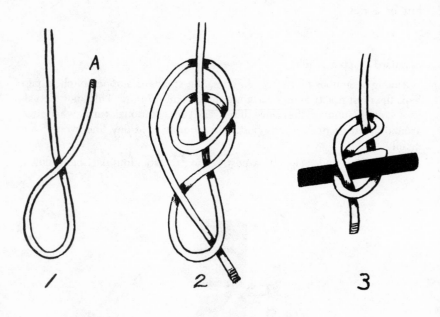

Tying. Loop end A *over* the standing part as in Figure 1; then bring it around *behind* the standing part, *over* the standing part and bight and *behind* the standing part again. Tuck the end down through the original loop, as in Figure 2. Pull taut. A toggle may be inserted, as in Figure 3. This makes the knot easy to untie.

KNOTS FOR JOINING TWO ENDS OF ROPE

Square Knot

The square knot, also known as the reef knot, is much in use because it is an excellent, useful knot which serves many purposes and holds well. It is also the principal knot used in first aid because it lies flat. Pliny, around A.D. 60, praised the reef knot, the "medical" knot, as he called it, for its use in tying bandages.

Though a square knot is often used to join the ends of two ropes of equal size, there are other knots and bends for this purpose which join more securely. This knot is commonly used for tying parcels. It ties and unties easily.

The square knot is used in square knotting techniques to weave many useful and decorative things, such as belts and bags.

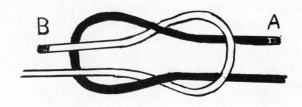

Tying. Look closely at the drawing for a moment or two; then bring end A over end B, toward you, under, and away from you. Now bring end B over A, away from you, under, and toward you. Pull the rope taut.

Surgeon's Knot

Surgeons use this ligature knot to assure sufficient friction to hold the first crossing until the second one can be tied. It is because of the possibility that catgut or silk will slip or loosen that the surgeon takes the extra turn or turns in making the lower (first) half of the square knot when tying the ligature, or surgeon's knot.

This knot is also known as the package knot, since the extra turn or two prevents the twine's slipping.

Tying. This knot (above) is tied in the same way as the square knot except that an extra turn or two is made with end A; the upper part is tied as in the square knot, then pulled taut. Some surgeons make an extra turn or two in the upper half of the knot as well.

Thief Knot

This is a knot which looks so much like the square knot that if the ends are covered, even a seasoned sailor cannot tell which is which. There is a yarn that sailors used the thief knot to discover if someone had rummaged in their ditty bags. Someone doing so in a hurry would certainly not notice that the bag had been secured by a thief knot instead of a square knot.

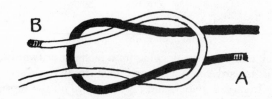

Tying. Make a bight in end B, then weave end A *up* through the bight, around B's end and standing part, then tuck end A *down* through the bight and pull taut. Note that the ends are *opposite* each other and the standing parts also, whereas in the square knot, the ends are on the *same* side of the knot and the standing parts are on the same side. If the knotter covers the ends with each hand, a person who looks at the knot would most likely mistake it for the square knot.

Granny Knot

This is a dangerous knot, especially when it is tied by a seafarer or camper to hold or take a strain. This knot is classed as dangerous because one never knows whether it will jam, or *slip*, instead of holding, as real knots do. It is doubly dangerous because it is generally tied unintentionally when a novice camper or boatman is trying to make a square knot. However, the granny knot on a bight is useful.

This is one knot for which no instructions are given here. A sure way to recognize this knot, before it is too late, is to examine this drawing carefully and note that in the square knot, one end and standing part goes *over* the bight at one end, and the other end and standing part goes *under* the bight at the other end. In the granny knot, at each end, the end and standing part cross on *different* sides of the bight.

Another *sure* way to spot a granny knot in a rope is that the knot will *not lie flat* when it is pulled tight.

Sheet Bend

The sheet bend, also known as the weaver's knot, is a fine knot with which to join two ropes of unequal size as well as the same size.

The Incas of Peru used the same sheet bend that we tie today, in weaving their fishnets—so did the Stone-Age Lake Dwellers!

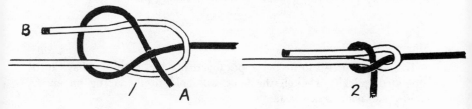

Tying. This knot is tied in much the same way as the square knot. First, tie a square knot, when practicing a sheet bend, then pass end A *under* its standing part and *over* the bight of the other rope, and pull taut. Or, the end of the other rope (B) is passed *over* its standing part and *under* the bight of the other rope, then pulled taut. After one has practiced a few times, the sheet bend can be tied directly. When pulled taut, this knot looks quite unlike the square knot. See Figure 2.

Another way to tie the sheet bend is to make a bight in end B, bring end A *up* through it and around it, then tuck end A under its own standing part.

Double Sheet Bend

Everyone who can tie the basic sheet bend can tie this knot, despite the slight difference in tying this bend. It is an excellent knot to use when bending two ropes of different size, but the larger rope should always be used for the bight or loop.

Tying. In the left hand, form a bight in the heavier rope, end B. Then bring end A, the thinner rope or cord, *up* through the bight and around it twice before tucking the end under its standing part.

Slippery Sheet Bend

This knot is useful to tie two ropes together when they may have to be separated quickly. Though the knot will hold firmly, a tug on end A causes it to come apart instantly.

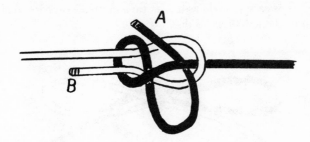

Tying. Make a bight in end B (the left-hand rope) and bring end A *up* through it, and around it. Then, make a bight in end A and pull it through *under* its own standing part.

Weaver's Knot

This is essentially the sheet bend, used for the same purpose, with a slight difference in the weaving of the ropes forming the knot. Weavers use it for joining their threads, when all of them in the warp break. The authors favor the sheet bend.

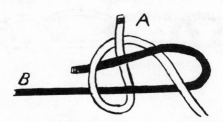

Tying. Make a bight in end B. Pass end A *down* through B's bight, then completely around B's end and standing part, and up between B's end and its own standing part, as illustrated.

Shoelace Knot

This knot is as easy to undo as it is to tie and, when properly tied, it will stay put throughout the entire day.

Tying. This is perhaps the best and easiest way to tie shoelaces. First, make an overhand loop. Then, make a bight on each side, another overhand loop with the bights, and the knot is tied.

When this knot is tied like the square knot, it will stay tied. If it is tied like the granny, however, it will come undone.

If the shoelaces are too long, a second shoelace knot can be made over the first.

Hawser Bend

This practical hitch can be tied in several ways. It is used for joining two lines as well as thick rope. It can be made with two half hitches or one, as illustrated. The ends are seized.

Tying. Make a bight and one or two half hitches (see page 54) in end A, then seize the end. Pass the end of rope B through bight A, then make one or two half hitches and seize end B.

Bowline Bend

This bend, formed by two interlocked bowline bights, is often used to bend two hawsers together when absolute security is necessary. They will not pull apart and the hawsers united may be of different sizes, without affecting the efficiency of the bend.

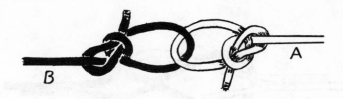

Tying. Make a bowline (see page 75) in rope A, pass the end of rope B up through the bight, then make a bowline in rope B.

Reeving Line Bend

There is not as much elasticity in this bend as in the carrick bend, but it is a more compact knot which is useful when one is bending lines which must pass through small hawser pipes or a small towing chock, where bigger bends jam.

Tying. Make an overhand loop in the end of rope A, pass the end of rope B through it, then make an overhand loop in end B so that it encircles A's standing part. Seize the ends *well* to make this bend safe.

Carrick Bend

The carrick bend was used at an early date in Britain, and a design of this knot was used as a heraldic device by Hereward the Wake, who defied William the Conqueror, the invader from Normandy, in A.D. 1066. In his honor the knot was frequently called the Wake knot and is known to this day by that name.

There are a great number of carrick bends, used chiefly for bending hawsers together and in towing, where heavy cables are used. A good point about these knots is that they will not jam very hard, even under considerable strain, as will the sheet bend, for instance. The carrick bend is a pretty knot, much used in decorative work. The single carrick bend and the double carrick bend are two of the most useful knots in this group.

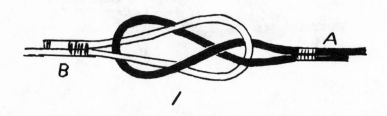

Tying. Single Carrick Bend: Make a bight in the end of rope B and seize it to its standing part. Then weave the end of rope A *up* through the bight B, across it, through where it is seized, around it, then *under* its own standing part and *over* bight B, as illustrated. Seize end A to its standing part. See Figure 1.

Double Carrick Bend: Make an underhand loop in rope B, then weave the end of rope A, as illustrated in Figure 2, by passing end A *under* the bight, through where it is seized, across the bight, *under* its own standing part, and *over* the bight. Seize.

Heaving Line Bend

This knot is used to bend a small rope to a larger one or to bend a heaving line to a hawser. It is a workmanlike bend which will hold without seizing.

Tying. Make a bight in the heavier rope, then pass the end of the smaller rope down through the bight and weave it around the larger rope, as illustrated. Finish by tucking the end of the smaller rope between itself and the larger rope.

Miller's Knot

This is the knot which millers use to fasten the mouths of grain sacks. Though it is a good knot for that purpose, the writers have found that the clove hitch does the job quite as well and is slightly easier to tie, since the two bights can be dropped easily and quickly over the gathering of the open end of the bag.

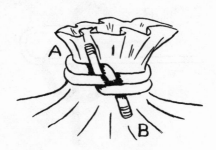

Tying. Place end B against the mouth of the sack; make a turn around the gatherings, cross the cord over end B and make a second turn below the first. Tuck end A up through the two turns, as illustrated.

Packer's Knot

This is an easily tied knot used for tying a package securely or for holding the wrapping on a parcel. The basic knot is the figure-of-eight, as can be seen in the drawing.

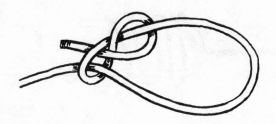

Tying. Make a figure-of-eight knot around the standing part, forming a running loop. The end should be parallel to the standing part. Place the loop around the package or parcel and pull it tight, then pass the string in the opposite direction, so that all four sides are secured. Finish it off with overhand or other knots.

Binder-Twine Bend

Farmers frequently use this knot for joining twine which must pass easily through binder machinery. For this reason, the two ends of this knot face in the same direction.

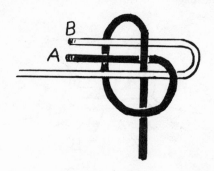

Tying. Make a bight in end B, the left-hand rope or twine, and bring end A (the right-hand rope) *up* through the bight, behind B's end and standing part, over its own standing part, *over* B's bight, and through its own bight. Pull taut.

True Lover's Knot

This fisherman's knot in disguise, also known as the Englishman's bend, is often regarded in England as the true lover's knot. This belief is opposed to the one which asserts that the true lover's knot was lost to posterity.

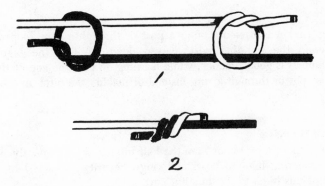

Tying. Tie two overhand knots, back to back, as in Figure 1, and snug, as in Figure 2.

HITCHES AND KNOTS USED FOR TYING ROPES TO THINGS

As a general rule, hitches are usually tied around something and are sometimes temporary fastenings which can be undone quickly. Other hitches will hold indefinitely, especially when seized to the standing part. Basic hitches are used for so many useful ties that they form an important part of a knot-tyer's repertoire. Often hitches are not actually tied in the hands but are hitched directly around a spar or object. One should learn to tie some of the hitches by using *both* ends of a rope, instead of forming a loop or loops in the standing part of the rope. This applies to hitches like the clove hitch, which cannot always be dropped over a mooring post or spar. Most hitches are easier to tie than many other knots. Some of the most useful hitches are described and illustrated in these pages.

Half Hitch

As the name implies, this is only half of a hitch. It is one of the easiest knots to tie. It is very useful because it is a basic formation of rope, on which other hitches are built or with which they are used in conjunction. One half hitch is of little use unless the end is stopped down (seized) to hold it secure.

Tying. End A is passed around a post or through a ring, looped under and around the standing part, passed down through the bight, then pulled taut. It is good practice, while learning, to pass the end of the hitch around a spar or through a ring instead of making the hitch in the hands.

Two Half Hitches

This is a more useful knot than the half hitch and is frequently used for securing mooring lines to posts and rings. Security is assured by seizing the end of this hitch to its standing part.

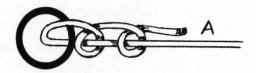

Tying. This hitch is tied in exactly the same way as the half hitch except that a second half hitch is made around the standing part, as shown in the drawing.

Round Turn and Two Half Hitches

The round turn and two half hitches are handy and secure for mooring a boat. The extra turn lessens the wear and tear on the rope. A round turn with the second half hitch stopped down (seized) is safe for mooring for long periods, and slack on the line has no effect on the security of the mooring.

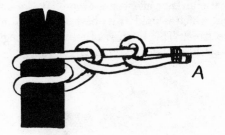

Tying. Place the standing part on the left of the mooring post, end A on the right, then loop A around the post so that it returns to its original position. Make two half hitches to complete the knot. Pull the line taut.

Canoe Hitch

The canoe hitch, also called the slippery hitch or slippery half hitch, is a very old knot. The Indians of the Northwest Coast of the United States and Canada used this knot as a finishing knot, tied last, on the lashings which held a maul head in place. They also used this hitch to fasten a

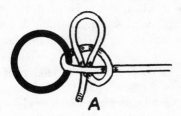

pony or to moor a canoe or boat, so that they could cast off in a hurry. The Eskimos, too, used this knot for various purposes. Though that was in the past, one can still see many of their boats and canoes moored to posts by the canoe hitch.

Tying. The end A is passed down through the ring and brought up over and around its standing part so that a bight is formed, as illustrated. The end of the canoe hitch can be prevented from pulling through by tying a simple overhand knot in the end or tucking it down through the bight.

Clove Hitch

This is a very useful knot afloat and ashore. It is a snug-holding, near-nonslipping hitch, which is used at its best around an upright spar, mast, tent pole, or tree trunk. This hitch is often used to begin or end various lashings, and to hitch a small rope to a larger rope.

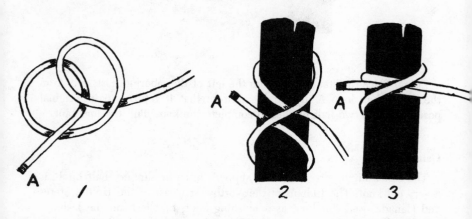

Tying. This knot is actually two half hitches, tied in a way that will grip firmly the object to which it is to be fixed. In tying it, place the rope around a post with end A on the right. Bring A over the standing part, around the post again and through, under its bight, as illustrated. Pull the rope taut.

To drop the loops of a ready-made clove hitch over the top of a mooring post, holding end A in the left hand, form an underhand loop, then an overhand loop right next to it. Place the second loop on top of the first and drop them both over the post. Pull taut. The hitch is secured by one or two half hitches tied on top of it.

This is a good place to point out that when two sections of rope cross each other, when a knot is being made, one must go *over* and the other *under*. Otherwise, wrong or useless knots are the result of mistaken sequence.

Rolling Hitch

This hitch is a modification of the clove hitch and is an effective knot, provided a strain is kept on it. If the rope is allowed to slack, or if it is jerked, the knot is liable to work loose. The double turn, being jambed by the hauling part, will not slip.

Tying. This knot is tied in the same way as the clove hitch, then end A is given an additional turn around the post between the other two turns, and is brought under the diagonal section, as illustrated.

Lark's Head

The single lark's head hitch is useful for fastening baggage labels to baggage and for "hitching up" animals. It can be tied by using either the ends of the rope, passing them through a ring or baggage handle, or by forming this hitch in the bight of a rope. The use of a toggle with a lark's head is shown under "Toggled Knots," in this chapter.

Tying. Make a bight in the rope or twine, pass it through a ring or a

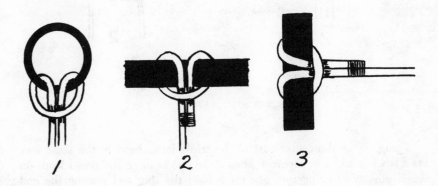

hole in the baggage tag, then bring the rope ends through the bight, as in Figure 1.

To hitch an animal to a rail, make twin loops in the rope, as in Figure 2, and seize the end or make two half hitches. To hitch it to a post, make twin loops in the rope, so that the standing part on each side is behind the rope; then place the right-hand loop on top of the left-hand loop and drop them over a post, as in Figure 3. This hitch may also be used for mooring a boat. To prevent the lark's head from slipping, the end may be seized to the standing part, as shown in the drawing.

Triple Lark's Head

In making decorative hitches, one can use a series of interlocking lark's heads, ranging from three to nine or more, based on the length of the rope, which actually form a chain around the ring or bar to which they are hitched.

Tying. Make the center part of the triple lark's head in the same way as a lark's head, as in Figure 1; then make one or more additional loops on each side by bringing the rope up behind the ring and passing the end down through the bight, as in Figure 2.

Timber Hitch

The timber hitch is an old knot which was used a good deal by the American Indians. It is easily and quickly tied and will not easily loosen when the strain is slackened.

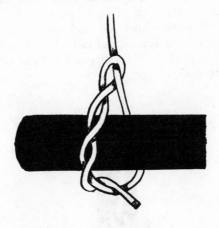

Tying. One end of the rope is passed around a pole, brought over and around its standing part, then turned three or four times back on itself, as shown in the drawing. The rope is then pulled taut.

Timber Hitch and Half Hitch

This knot was used chiefly to pull logs, poles, and branches along the ground or to tow them in the water, and is also used to hoist spars, logs, and other lengthy objects. The half hitch, made fast close to the end of the log or spar being pulled, is needed to hold it on a straight course, and will also direct the end of the spar being hoisted in an upright position.

Tying. First, tie a regular timber hitch, then tie a half hitch near the end of the spar, to hold it on its course, as illustrated.

Lifting Hitch

This useful hitch, also known as the well-pipe hitch, was used mainly to hoist cylindrical objects, such as pipes, masts, and heavy poles, into position. A half hitch or other hitch was made in the standing part of the rope when the object being hoisted had to be held in a vertical position. This hitch can also be used to make a rope fast to a tree or stake, when the rope is under great strain.

Tying. Working from top to bottom, make several turns around the pipe, as shown in the drawing, and finish the hitch with two half hitches around the standing part, as shown.

Barrel Sling

This hitch is useful mainly for hoisting a barrel with an open end by means of a derrick or other hoist. Once the sling has been made, it may be used as often as needed, without undoing any of its parts. When the hitch is being used to hoist a metal cylinder or some object which is slippery, it is wise to make two loops, instead of one, around the object being hoisted.

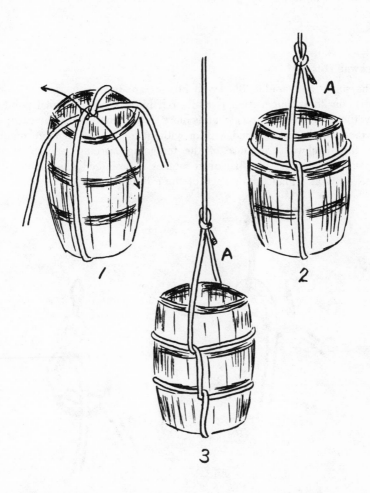

Tying. Place the barrel upright on a length of strong rope that is about three times as long as the height of the barrel from end A. Bring the ends up over the top of the barrel and tie them, as in Figure 1, in an overhand knot. Pull the ropes where they cross, in the direction indicated by the arrows, bringing them down on each side, as in Figure 2. Bring end A up and tie a bowline on the standing part.

If the barrel is slippery, pass two loops around it, as in Figure 3.

Blackwall Hitches

The single and double Blackwall hitches are invariably shown in any treatise on knots, *but* neither is really reliable from a functional point of view, though the double Blackwall is more so than the single. The cats-paw and the lark's head knot, tied with or without toggle, are far more reliable than the Blackwalls. Because of the foregoing warning, neither of the simple ways of tying the Blackwall hitches is described, though the diagrams show at a glance how each of these hitches is tied.

Bill Hitch

This method of hitching a rope onto a hook is done in the manner of a sheet bend, as the diagram shows. In this case, the bend is not used to bend two ropes together, as usual.

Cat's-Paw

The cat's-paw is used to hitch a sling or other continuous rope to a hook. This is a far safer hitch than the above-mentioned ones.

Tying. This may be tied by forming two loops, one in each hand, with the ends hanging inside the bight and behind it, as when preparing a lark's head with toggle. Turn the loops inward two or three times, making complete turns each time, then hang them side by side over the hook to which they are to be attached.

Mousing

A hook should be moused when the rope in it has to be held in place for some time. When rope tackles are allowed to slacken, there is always the chance that the rope will jump out of the hook. To prevent this, several turns around the bill and back of the hook should be made with a piece of twine or thin cord.

A few frapping turns are then made around the turns to draw them tight, and the ends are square-knotted together. The illustration shows just how to mouse.

Fisherman's Bend

Few knots combine more strength and simplicity than this bend. It will neither slip nor jam under strain and can be untied easily. When no tension is put on this knot, it is liable to slip, but this is easily corrected by seizing the end to the standing part. This is also called the anchor bend.

Tying. Pass end A around a pole, through a ring, or around a stone, for an anchor, making two turns around the object. Then bring end A *down* over the standing part and *up* through the loops. Make a second half hitch, as shown.

Killick Hitch

This hitch, based on the timber hitch, is a good way to secure a heavy stone or piece of metal on the end of a line to form a temporary mooring. The pull on this hitch assures the necessary tension to make the boat fast.

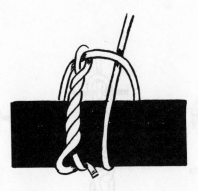

Tying. Be sure to leave enough rope to work with, depending on the diameter of the object. Make a turn, pass the end over the standing part, then make another turn in the opposite direction and loop it over the bight formed. Turn the rope around itself several times, as illustrated. Pull taut.

Belaying

When a landlubber makes a rope fast to a cleat or around a belaying pin, he uses too much rope to make too many needless turns.

Tying. One turn around the cleat, then two figure-of-eight knots, followed by a snugged hitch, will hold as long as the rope holds. The drawing shows how to begin the knot.

TOGGLED KNOTS

Toggles are pencil-shaped lengths and thicknesses of wood or metal which are used with various knots and hitches, such as the lark's head, the chain knot, and the sheepshank, illustrated, to prevent the rope from binding

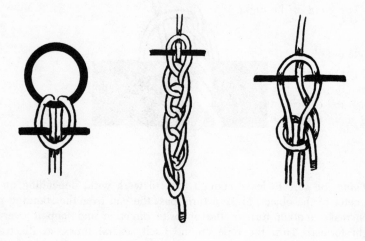

and to make releasing the hitches easier. Once the toggle is removed, the knot is either loose or the hitch falls apart, instantly, when the toggle is slid out.

Lark's Head With Toggle

A lark's head brought over a ring or bar, with a toggle slipped into place, as illustrated, is a most useful knot for suspending a weighty object or fastening anything when there is a pull on the rope. Only a small amount of strain is necessary to hold the toggle in place, and it can be withdrawn at a moment's notice, instantly releasing the knot.

Tying. Slip a bight through a metal ring or over a bar, then slip the toggle *in front of* the bight and *behind* the two falls of rope, as shown.

Toggle Bend

This is a very useful knot when the eyes (bights) of two ropes have to be fastened together. As will be seen, a toggle holds the two bights together and can be withdrawn in an instant. This toggle bend can be used for joining two small, bowline-type bights.

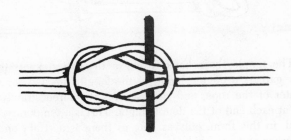

Tying. Slip one bight up through the other, then slip the toggle between the bight and standing parts, as shown.

SHORTENING ROPE

A seasoned sailor or real outdoorsman never shortens a rope by cutting it unless unusual circumstances force him to do so. If you will remember that a rope joined by knotting is a weak rope, you will want to use one of the following knots or hitches to shorten rope.

Sheepshank

A useful knot for shortening rope aboard ship or in camp, this is perhaps the best-known of rope shorteners. It has a double purpose, since it not only shortens rope but also strengthens it where needed, by adding two extra strands of rope where the rope is weak. In such cases, the weak part of the rope should be placed in the center of the slack forming the knot.

So many—more than thirty—forms of this knot have been known over the years, that it is not surprising that Captain John Smith, of Pocahontas fame, wrote that among the knots most used by the sailors of his time was the "sheepshanke."

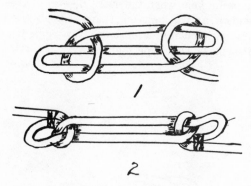

Tying. The simple sheepshank is one of the easiest knots to tie, since one simply gathers a double bight, of the lengths needed for shortening, in the center of the rope, and then secures the three strands by a half hitch, tied at each end of the double bight. This is a temporary knot, since it will hold, in this form, only as long as there is a strain on it to keep the half hitches taut.

There are many ways to hold this knot in place. One easy way is to slip a toggle or piece of wood through the loop at each end. A better way is to seize the end of each half hitch with a few turns of string or cord around the standing part, the seizing binding all three ropes, or only two, as shown in the drawing. The knot can also be made secure by tying an overhand knot over each bight.

The sheepshank tied on a "free-ended rope" is easily secured by knotting the free end, at each end, around the bight with an overhand knot or by the simple method of passing the free end through the bight, at each end.

Still another way to fasten the ends is by using a clove hitch instead of a half hitch over the bight at each end.

An overhand knot may be tied in the center before securing the ends.

Chain Knot

This knot, one of the types of twist knot for shortening a rope, is tied chiefly for its decorative effect. Actually, a sheepshank will do an equally effective job of shortening a line, and it is tied more easily.

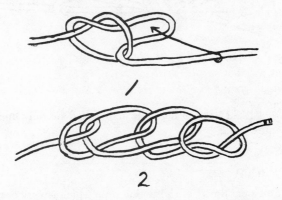

Tying. Make a slip knot (see page 78), and pull a bight down through it, as in Figure 1. Continue in this way, making as many "links" as desired, until the chain is the correct length. Then, push the end of the rope down through the final bight. Pull the rope taut.

Granny Knot on a Bight

Everyone knows that a granny knot has absolutely no use—except on a bight. This is a useful method of shortening rope, by putting two loops in its center or elsewhere on the bight.

Tying. Take a bight in each hand, as when tying a sheepshank, but tie two overhand knots in the center, one over the other.

Overhand Knot on a Bight

This knot is less bulky than the preceding knot.

Tying. Take a bight in each hand, as above, and tie only one overhand knot in the center.

Interlocking Hitch Weave

This is an ornamental way of shortening rope which is very easy to make.

Tying. This is simply a series of interlocking overhand loops, made as shown.

WHIPPING

Rope ends should be whipped to keep them from fraying and unraveling. A lit match held for an instant to the end of a nylon rope will do the job, but a different sort of whipping is required for ordinary rope. At sea, the ends of rope are often needle-whipped, to make certain that the turns do not unwind, but the usual method of whipping the end of a rope with a strong piece of twine is quite satisfactory. A 2-foot length of twine will prove ample for most jobs since, frequently, the whipping is made no wider than the diameter of the rope being whipped.

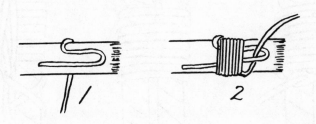

How to Whip

Place the string against the rope so that it forms a bight, as in Figure 1, then wind the string toward the end, as in Figure 2, and thread the end of the string up through the bight. The string should be touching but not overlapping on each side as it is wound, and the whipping should be about the diameter of the rope. When the whipping is complete, pull the end at the left so that the bight is brought under the whipping and the end is brought under with it. Snip off the ends.

SEIZINGS

Seizings either hold two parallel ropes together or form an eye. Seizing must be used on the carrick bends, among others. The two seizings most in use are the round seizing and the racking seizing. The first is made of frapping turns and two clove hitches, and the second is composed of an eye splice and a series of figure-of-eight turns, as illustrated.

Round Seizing

This seizing is more in use than the racking seizing.

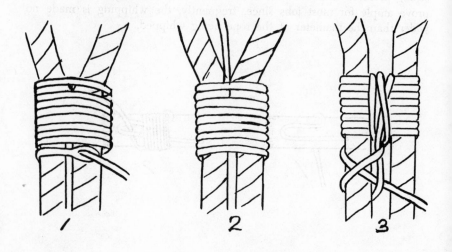

Tying. When seizing large rope, make an eye in one end of the seizing material, and when seizing small rope with twine, make a timber hitch to bring the two ropes or bight together. Loosely make about eight to ten turns, then pass the end down between the loops formed. Pass the end up through the eye and snug the loops, as in Figure 1. Make a second series of turns over the first, so that they rest in the grooves, where the first turns touch each other, but do not pull them so tight that they will separate the first turns. Tuck the end under, as in Figure 2. Make a clove hitch between the two ropes, then another clove hitch at the foot of the seizing, as in Figure 3.

Racking Seizing

When the strain is greater on one rope than on the other, the racking seizing is used.

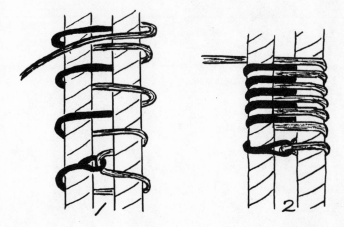

Tying. Starting with an eye splice (see page 108), make as many turns as desired. These turns are woven in a figure-of-eight pattern, as in Figure 1. When this set of turns is completed, wind the material back toward the eye splice, so that it fits into the empty spaces shown in Figure 2. These turns go round the ropes, as in a round seizing. The seizing may be finished in the same way as the round seizing, with clove hitches. (The figure-of-eight seizing is shown in black at the left so that it is easier to see how it is woven.)

Hitches and Knots, Plain and Fancy

This chapter contains hitches and knots which are utilitarian and also some of the ornamental sort. Knots for the fisherman, the camper, the trail rider, and the boatman are here, as are splicing, lashing, and similar outdoor arts which will prove almost equally useful in camp, at sea, or on the pack trail.

LOOP KNOTS

Over the centuries, several reliable forms of loop knots have been used by mountaineers, sailors, and outdoorsmen.

Bowline

The bowline, in its varied forms, is one of the best and most useful of this group of knots. It is one of the knots commonly used by sailors in the days of Captain John Smith who, writing of knots around 1620, mentioned the "boling" as among the most used knots aboard ship. It is used for hitching, hoisting, and hauling, and for mooring boats or bending ropes.

Whether tied by sailors, cowboys, or outdoorsmen, each in his own way, the outstanding feature of the bowline is that the knot is entirely dependable and will not slip or jam, even under great strain. This is all that can be asked of any knot. A few different ways of tying this knot are given in these pages.

Tying. The basic bowline is made with only one end of the rope. The knot is tied by leaving enough end loose to make a bowline loop of the size desired, such as round the waist. First, make a small loop, with the standing part on the under side, then bring the end *up* through the loop, around the standing part, and *down* through the loop.

Running Bowline

This is a fine temporary running knot which can convert a rope into a lasso. It may be tied as an actual knot, in order not to have to pass a long-standing part of rope through the loop of the basic bowline.

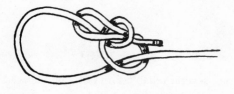

Tying. Make a regular bowline around the standing part by passing the end of the rope *under* and around the standing part before making a bowline, as explained above. However, this bowline should have a very small loop, since only the rope (standing part) has to run through it.

Double Bowline

This form of the knot is most useful in rescue work, or when one wants to work with both arms free. One may sit on one loop of this knot, while the other loop supports the body, giving the arms free play.

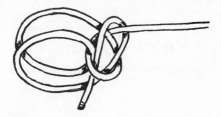

Tying. Start as though to make a bowline, but run the end *up* through the loop twice, before bringing it around the standing part and *down* through the loop. The drawing shows clearly how this is done.

Bowline on a Bight

This knot is used much less than the other forms of the bowline. It is made in the bight (center) of a doubled rope.

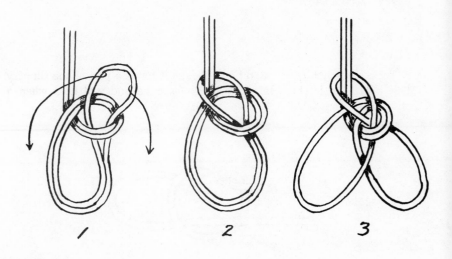

Tying. Using the doubled rope, start as for a simple bowline, pulling the bight *up* through the small loop, as in Figure 1; pull it *down* and around, so that it is *behind* the standing part, as in Figure 2. Spread the loops, as in Figure 3.

Spanish Bowline

This bowline is more easily tied by laying the rope on a flat surface and working on it in that position.

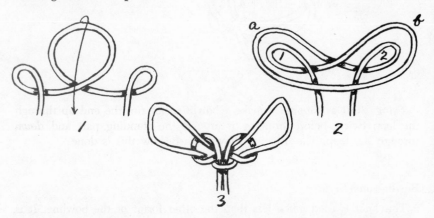

Tying. First, arrange the rope as in Figure 1, then bring the center loop down and arrange it as in Figure 2, so that it is large enough for the two small loops to fit inside. Then pull bight *a* though loop 1 and bight *b* through loop 2. Pull taut.

Slip Knot

This knot is not a very useful one, though it forms a part of the slippery half hitch, the hitching tie, and the shoelace tie and will hold when a strain is put on it.

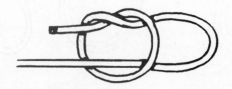

Tying. Hold one end of the rope in the left hand, then make an overhand loop in the standing part and pull a bight up through the loop. When tying this knot onto a rail or bar, put one end of the rope over the rail, then tie an overhand knot around the standing part.

Marlinspike Hitch

This is a useful knot for heaving a seizing taut and when leverage is required. The extreme simplicity with which this hitch can be tied and released in a flash is commendable.

Tying. Make a bight and pass the standing part behind it. Slip the marlinspike over the bight, *under* the standing part, and over the bight on the other side.

Man-Harness Knot

This knot, or rather a series of similar knots, is used for hauling or dragging, with a single rope, any heavy object which will roll or slide. The men who pull put one arm and shoulder through a loop, the loops being made far enough apart to allow free body movement. In some of these man-harness knots, strong, lightweight metal rings, about 6 inches in diameter, are fastened to the rope at suitable intervals, and the haulers pull by each tugging on a ring. The authors have used, far afield, versions of this knot, almost identically tied, in which *two* lines of pulling men and women were formed by tying *both* ends of the length of rope to the object being hauled. The double rows of harness loops were formed on both sides of the bight of the rope.

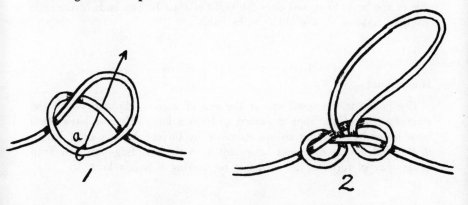

Tying. This knot is tied in the middle of the rope. First, form an under-hand loop and bring the standing part around, under the loop, as in Figure 1. Pull the rope, at point *a*, *under* the standing part and *over* the bight, as shown by the arrow. This will form a new, large bight. Pull the rope taut.

Gunner's Knot

This knot is similar to the man-harness knot and is used for the same purposes.

Tying. The rope is first passed through one or two rings, at the center, than an overhand loop is made, just below the rings, in the left-hand (B) rope. Another loop is made on the right-hand (A) rope by crossing it under the bight *over* B's standing part, then *under* the left side of the large loop which connects the two rings, *over* the bight of rope B, *under* the right side of the large loop, and *over* the bight of rope B. The ends of the rope are then fastened to the object to be hauled.

Honda Knot

The honda is the small eye at the end of a rope, through which the standing part of the rope is passed to form a lariat. Hondas have often been formed by making an eye splice or by turning back a short length of the end of the rope and whipping it to the standing part. An even easier way of forming the eyelet is by making a honda knot.

Tying. Make an overhand knot about 6 inches from the end of the rope, then pass the end through it, between the standing part and the bight, where the knot crosses. Tie a small overhand knot in the tip end, as a stopper knot, or seize the end to the standing part. To make a lariat, pass the other end of the rope through the honda.

Lineman's Loop

The lineman's loop is one of the best loops for tying in the standing part of a rope. It is fairly easily tied and it will not slip when pulled from either end, nor will it jam easily.

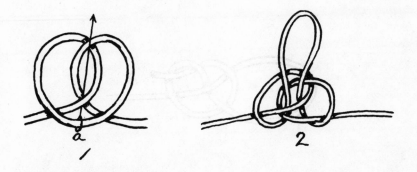

Tying. It is best to arrange the rope on a flat surface, as in Figure 1, with an overhand loop at the left and an underhand loop at the right.

Note that the loop at the right crosses *over* the other at the top and *under* it at the foot, where they cross, at the center. Pull point *a* up through the center and into a bight, as in Figure 2.

Eye Knot

This overhand knot on a bight is a very easily tied slip knot which will not pull loose. It is often used as a fisherman's tie and a mooring tie.

Tying. Make a bight and tie an overhand knot on it.

Crabber's Eye Knot

This knot is not often seen, though it does form a useful running eye with increased friction. It is also used as a finishing knot, when tied below a lark's head on a spar. It is easily tied, as shown by the drawing.

Tying. Make an underhand loop in end A, then bring the end over the standing part, *under* the left side of the bight, *over* the right side, then tuck the end *up* through its own bight.

Tom Fool Knot

This is like a bow knot, except for the final crossing of the ends. In the days of sail and brigs, old sailors used this knot as a trick, exhibition knot, tying it quickly, with a deceptive flourish, to amaze landlubbers and greenhorns in the crew. It had little practical use except for emergency handcuffs or as a sling for a jar.

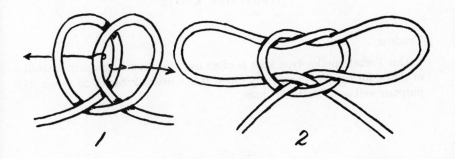

Tying. Make two loops, one overhand and the other underhand; as shown in Figure 1, the underhand loop overlaps the other. Pull the parts which overlap in the direction indicated by the arrows, and the bow in Figure 2 will be formed.

Handcuff Hitch

This hitch was used instead of iron shackles in the days of clipper ships. When the knot was snugged, by pulling the ends taut, the two ends were tied with a reef knot, holding a prisoner securely.

Tying. Working from left to right, make an underhand loop in end B, then a bight which crosses *under* then *over* the bights and under end B. Then make an overhand loop in end A, which passes *over* the bight and *under* the inside edge of the first loop and the bight, *over* its outer side, then *under* the bight, as illustrated.

STRETCHER KNOTS

Tendeur

This French, pulley-type knot is often used by French campers, instead of slides, for tightening tent guy ropes. It is a useful knot which serves its purpose well as a "stretcher" knot.

Tying. An overhand knot is made two or three feet from the end of the guy line. The end of the rope is then brought around the tent peg, then through the overhand knot, as illustrated. Another overhand knot is made over the standing part, at the end of the rope, as illustrated.

Poulie

This pulley knot, of French origin, is used by campers and woodsmen to stretch strongly or hold something in position, and to haul heavy objects, with a stout rope.

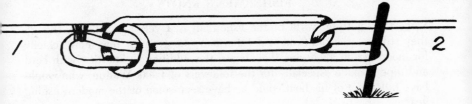

Tying. The weight is at point 1 and the pull (traction) at point 2. Make a loop, as shown in the drawing, and a bight two feet or more away from it. Make a second bight, near point 1, and pass it through the loop and seize it, as illustrated. Pass the free part of the rope around a stout stake, driven firmly into the ground, and up through the first (upper) bight, as shown.

Taut Line Hitch

Since the taut line hitch will slide only one way, it is frequently used on tent guys, in the place of slides. This hitch will also hold more firmly than the clove hitch on slippery poles.

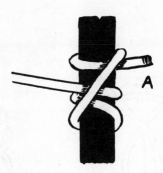

Tying. Place end A around a pole, make a turn below it, then bring it up across the standing part, around the pole, and tuck the end through, as illustrated.

FISHERMEN'S KNOTS

Since the knotting world of the fisherman is a very special one, though they still use the old-fashioned fisherman's knot and a few more, chiefly for mooring and anchoring their boats, this addition to knotting with cord and rope is made especially for the followers of Izaak Walton, who would have fallen out of his boat could he have seen some of the modern fishing gear.

Knotting With Monofilament

Making knots with monofilament is a craft in itself! This is chiefly because of joins, splices, bends, and loops which have to be made in gut and monofilament, some of which are nearly invisible strands, hardly thicker than those in a spider's web. A few of these knots are dealt with here, but many cannot be adequately described or illustrated on paper. There is one major piece of advice, covering practically all ties made with monofilament. It applies not only to spin fishermen but also to all who tie monofilament knots: Never make less than five or more turns around the standing part of the line.

Fisherman's Eye Knot

This knot is generally used to fasten the bight of a gut leader to a fishing line.

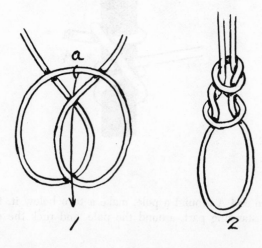

Tying. Make twin loops, and place the inside edge of the right loop *over* the left, as in Figure 1; pull point *a* down through the center, as indicated by the arrow. This will result in an overhand knot on each side, as in Figure 2. Pull taut.

Figure-of-Eight Knot

This knot is well-liked because it permits the hook to hang at the correct angle and is easily tied and untied.

Tying. Thread the gut through the eye. Bring the end behind and around the hook, *under* the standing part, then *over* it, and tuck the end down through the bight, as illustrated. Pull taut.

Blood Knot

This is a knot used for joining fish lines and nylon leaders. It holds well.

Tying. Make two turns on line B with end A, then tuck end A *down* between its standing part and B. Make two turns on line A with end B and tuck the end *up* between A's standing part and its own. Pull taut.

Fisherman's Knot

This is an efficient knot (also called the smooth knot) for attaching filament or nylon leaders; it is easily tied, as the drawing shows.

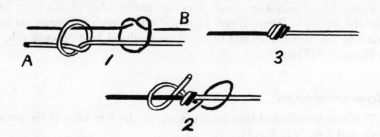

Tying. Make an overhand knot near the end of line A, pass the end of line B through it and make an overhand knot on line B. Snug and make a half hitch at each end. Pull taut.

Turtle Knot

This is a good, secure knot for attaching hook, spinner, or fly to a nylon or gut leader.

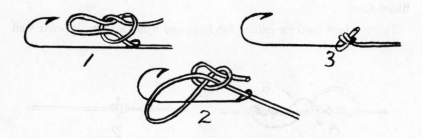

Tying. Thread the gut through the eye, make an overhand knot over a bight, then pull the bight down over the hook. Pull taut.

Clinch Knot

This is another good knot for fastening a fly or a hook to a leader, at any point, with the certainty that it will stay put.

Tying. Thread the gut through the eye, make a bight and five twists toward you, then slip the bight over the hook. Pass the end through the bight. Pull taut.

Jam Hitch

This type of loop knot is used by many fishermen because of its simplicity and effectiveness. The knot on the end of the line jams tightly when the knot is pulled tight, but the knot is easily untied.

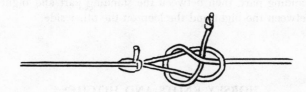

Tying. Thread the gut *up* through the bight and around it, then tuck the end between its own standing part and the bight. Make an overhand knot at the very end.

Wedge Knot

This is a knot of the clinch school, excellent for tying a filament leader to hook, fly, or spinner.

Tying. Thread the gut through the eye, pass the end behind and over the standing part twice, then pass it behind the standing part again and tuck the end through the bight, as illustrated.

Compound Knot

This knot is not so difficult as it looks. It is an excellent knot for making a loop in the end of a filament or other leader.

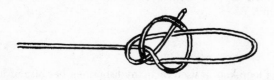

Tying. Make an overhand loop and pull a bight through it. Pass the end over the standing part, then between the standing part and bight on one side and between the bight and the loop on the other side.

HORSEY KNOTS AND HITCHES

The following knots and hitches are all connected in some way with horses.

Hackamore

Probably this rope bridle was first used in North America by the Indians. For this reason it is still known as the Indian bridle knot. Variations of this knot are used as jar and jug slings.

Tying. The illustrations of how this knot is tied are probably easier to follow than a written description. First, make a bowline at one end of the rope and pass the other end through the bight. (The rope need not be longer than about twelve feet, for use in the stall, though a longer rope may be used if desired. The loop in the bowline should be small.) Pass the running loop thus formed over the horse's head so that it fits around the animal's neck. Then, make two half hitches, as shown in Figure 1, placing the loops over the horse's nose. Tuck the second loop *down* through the first, as in Figure 2, then pull it up over the horse's ears. Tuck the free end of rope through the bight, at the nose, as in Figure 3.

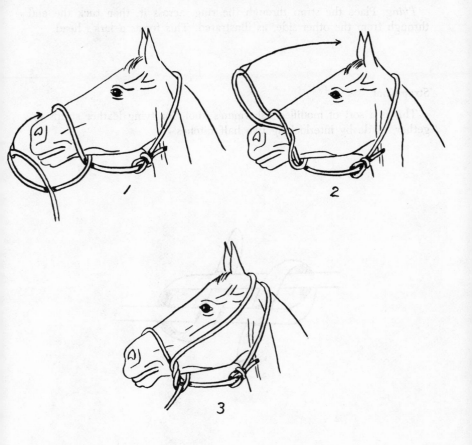

Girth Hitch

This knot is also for use around horses. It is the easiest and best way to fasten a rope or leather strap to a metal ring. It is used chiefly for hitching the cinch strap of a Western saddle.

Tying. Place the strap through the ring, across it, then tuck the end through from the other side, as illustrated. This forms a lark's head.

Strap Knot

This is a sort of modified fisherman's knot, for tying leather straps together, made by interlocking two half hitches.

Tying. The drawing shows exactly how this simple knot is made.

Diamond Hitch

This somewhat complex hitch is "thrown" by packtrain men, trappers, and traders, to hold baggage and packs on packhorses and mules. It is a very effective hitch, more so than any other hitch used for a similar purpose. Its big advantage is that strain on any part of the rope causes the line to tighten along its entire length. Often, packers use a ring on one end of the rope and a hook on the other end.

This is an excellent and effective hitch to use on some pack frames, ones on which the rope may be passed behind six projecting parts of the pack frame, a six-point job.

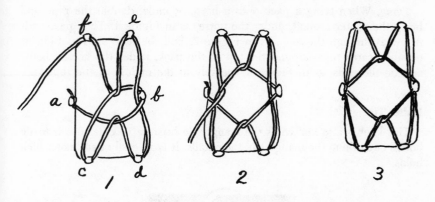

Tying. When using a diamond hitch on a pack frame, first tie a clove hitch at point *a*, shown in Figure 1. Then loop the rope over around points *b* and *c*. Leave the center loop fairly loose since it will form the diamond. Pull the rope *down* through the loop and around point *d*, *up* through the loop at *b*, around *e*, and *down* through the upper part of the loop and around *f*. By now, the loop is becoming diamond-shaped. Pull the rope *up* through the diamond near point *a*, as in Figure 2, then pull the rope taut to tighten all sides of the hitch. Tie the rope end by a hitch or knot to point *a*. Figure 3 shows the completed hitch with the diamond at the center.

If trying a pack onto a horse or mule, point *a* is generally a ring in one end of the girth, and point *b* the hook in the other end. Otherwise, the hitch is tied in the same way.

Squaw Hitch

This is another good packing hitch, originally devised by Indian squaws, who were not up to inventing the diamond hitch. They used their hitch for tying packs onto the backs of dogs and horses and for fastening bundles onto the travois. This hitch serves well on the packtrain trail and can be made more easily than the diamond hitch. The squaw hitch can also be used for tying packs onto frames.

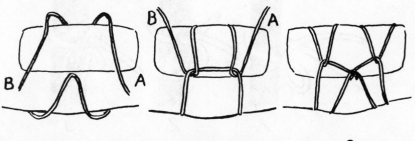

Tying. When tying a pack onto a horse or mule, double the rope and bring the center around, under the horse, as in Figure 1. Then pass ends A and B through the loop, as in Figure 2. Pull the rope ends as tight as possible, carry them around the top of the pack, under the horse's belly, and tie the ends, as in Figure 3, securely to the middle of the rope.

Halter Tie

This knot is also known as the manger tie because its chief use is to tie horses or cattle to the mangers in their stalls. It is an easily tied knot which holds.

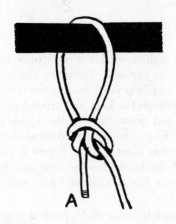

Tying. Pass end A through a ring or around a rail, bring it *down* and around the standing part, then *up* and across the bight formed, and tuck it down through, as illustrated.

Hitching Tie

This is one of a number of knots and hitches used for tethering animals. It is an easy and effective knot which can be untied in a flash.

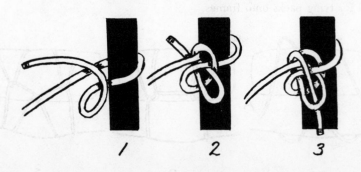

1   2   3

Tying. Take a turn around a post, then make a loop, as in Figure 1, leaving enough end to pull it over the standing part and make a bight through the loop, as in Figure 2. Then, pull the rope end *down* across the loop and tuck it down under the bight, as in Figure 3.

Horse Hitch

This easily tied knot is a lark's head knot, tied around a pole. It is also known as the cow hitch. It is not quite dependable unless it is finished off with a single or double half hitch. The hitching tie above is a more reliable hitch.

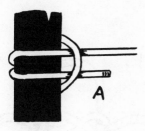

Tying. Place end A around a post, forming a bight on the side by bringing the end down over the standing part, then make a second turn below the first, in the opposite direction and tuck the end through the bight. Pull taut. One or two half hitches will make this a better knot.

DECORATIVE KNOTS

Many so-called "knots," in medieval times, were not actual knots but designs used as and on heraldic devices.

There are countless forms of decorative knots, some having only a heraldic or other significant meaning, while the remainder are almost entirely decorative, though some, such as the Wake knot, known today as the carrick bend, serve various everyday purposes, in addition to looking pretty. Some of the latter are illustrated, and the method of tying them is given elsewhere in this book.

Heraldic Knots

Such knots were embroidered on the surcoats of knights to denote personal or family emblems. Later, these coats, worn over their armor, became known as coats of arms. A number of these knots were used as the badge of a royal, religious, or other prominent house. Some kings and popes used knots as emblems. The royal House of Savoy used a double-strand figure-of-eight knot as the family emblem, coupled with the motto, "It bends, but binds not."

Three of these knots, which have no practical value but are decorative, are illustrated here. No instructions are given for tying them because of their lack of utility, but they may be tied without difficulty by simply studying the drawings.

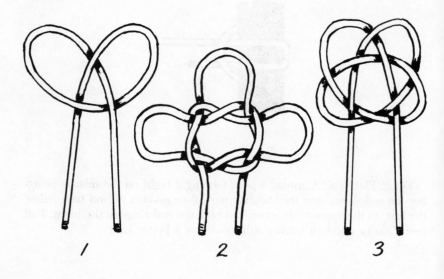

Figure 1 is the Staffordshire knot, Figure 2, the shamrock, and Figure 3, the Napoleon's knot.

Decorative Sword Knot

In days gone by, various forms of bends were intertwined to make ornamental sword knots. One of these knots is illustrated, of special interest

since it is a facsimile of the knot used on the sword of gold presented by
Louis XVI of France to General George Washington during the American

Revolution. It was also the knot used on the sword presented by the
Colonial Army to the Marquis de Lafayette as a means of paying tribute
and saying "Thanks!"

As will be seen from the drawing, the knot was made by interlocking
two carrick bends on a loop.

True Shamrock Knot

This decorative knot is easy to tie. From it, the pretty flower knot, which
is no less ornamental, can be made. The true shamrock knot, doubled, described below, is another form of the true shamrock tie.

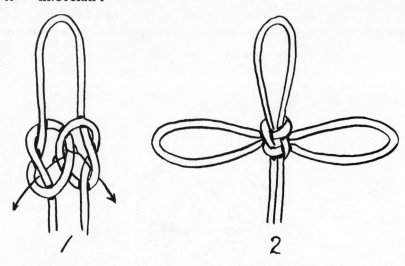

Tying. Make two interlacing overhand knots, as in Figure 1, and pull the bights in opposite directions and through the overhand knots, as indicated by the arrows. Pull taut and make the three loops formed of equal length, as in Figure 2.

True Shamrock Knot Doubled

This knot is tied the same as the true shamrock knot, only with two lengths of cord. It is perhaps more decorative than the other.

Flower Knot

This delicate little five-petaled flower is easily evolved from the true shamrock knot.

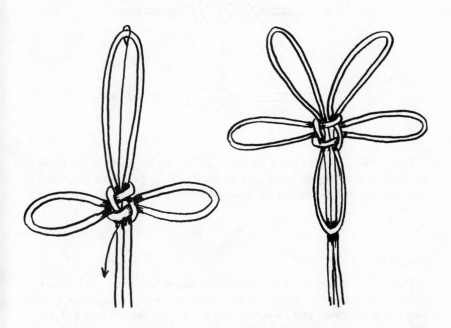

Tying. First, tie the true shamrock knot, but make the top loop about twice as large as the others. When the knot is complete, bring the top loop down under the two horizontal cords in the center of the knot, as in Figure 1, so that the loop passes through the body of the knot. It will now be at the bottom, forming the lower petal and there will be two new loops at the top. This will form a five-petaled flower, as in Figure 2.

Capuchin Knot

This is a useful, unusual knot, of French origin. It was used by the Capuchin order of monks on the end of the cords which hung from their cord belts. This knot can be made with as many as six turns—more if one is a "knotsman"—in soft, suitable cord or nylon rope. The art of tying the knot is to make the loop disappear completely into the body of the knot.

This knot can be used to decorate lanyards or as a stopper knot, though it seems almost too pretty to use for that purpose.

The Peruvian Incas used an almost identical knot in their quipus to indicate numbers. The Incas, however, always left the loop outside the turns, without merging it with them.

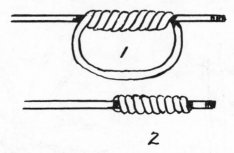

Tying. Make a small bight near the end of the cord and make three to six turns around the standing part, as shown. Then pull both the standing part and the end to tighten the knot, and make the bight merge with the turns.

Parade Loop

This is the decorative knot which one sees when the proud horses of cavalry and police trot past in review. Rope and knot are as white as pipe clay can make them, and each knot has exactly the same number of turns. The loop is easy to make and is also used as a lanyard knot, around a person's neck instead of a horse's. This is also known as the hangman's noose.

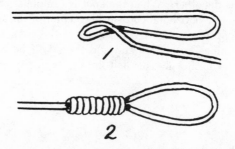

Tying. Take a bight in one hand, leaving about 2 feet of rope hanging loose. Double the rope back to form a small bight, as in Figure 1, then make a series of turns, *away* from you, working downward around the two ropes, toward the small (lower) bight. Tuck the rope end through the small bight and pull the upper bight taut, as in Figure 2. The rope end should lie flat against the lowest turn where it is practically invisible. In soft rope, the end disappears inside the turns.

LANYARD KNOTS

A three-strand Turk's head or a four-strand Turk's head, or an English diamond knot is often used on a lanyard.

Three-Strand Turk's Head

A Turk's head is both decorative and useful on a lanyard.

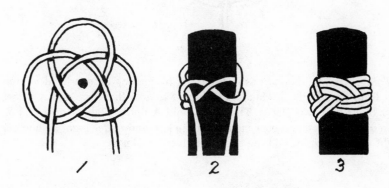

Tying. Arrange the cord as in Figure 1, then place the center (marked by a black dot in the diagram) over a dowel, pencil, or other small, cylindrical object, as in Figure 2. Weave the ends, following the arrangement in Figure 2, until each part of the knot has three strands. Tie the ends securely so that they are hidden inside the knot.

The Turk's head may also be used for decoration flattened out, as below.

English Diamond Knot

This knot is useful on the looped end of a lanyard; it is also used to decorate other objects.

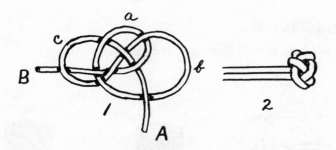

Tying. Arrange the cord as in Figure 1, by making an overhand loop at end B, to form bight *a*. Make bight *b* next to *a* so that rope end A passes *over* bight *a* in two places. Then bring end A under bight *b over* end B, then *under* bight *a* and *over* bight *b*, at the left, and *under* bight *a* and *over* bight *b*, at the right. Pull the ends to tighten the knot.

LASHING

This is not a difficult skill to acquire, but care has to be taken to make a lashing which is neat and tight, with the ends snug. Each turn in the lashing must be drawn tight and kept so close to the others that it touches them without overlapping. The hitches, often the clove hitch or timber hitch, which start and end lashings, should be tied tightly and begun and finished at the correct point on the poles being lashed. Lashings are used for joining ropes and in different forms of rigging, but the main purpose is for lashing poles and spars together in various ways. Three of the most useful lashings of this sort are square lashing, diagonal lashing, and shear lashing.

The way of binding lashings together is called frapping.

Frapping

This is the method of drawing two slack lines tightly together with a short length of rope, which is then fastened with a square, or reef, knot. The turns of a pole lashing are also bound together by a few frapping turns, in order to make the lashing very snug. The drawing shows how these turns are made.

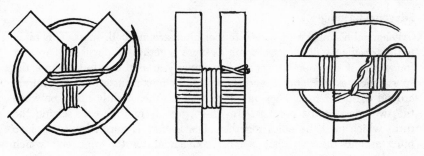

Square Lashing

A clove hitch is tied on the upright spar so that the long end of the lashing rope pulls straight out from the hitch. The horizontal spar is placed directly above the hitch. The rope is then taken upward in front of and over the horizontal spar. It now passes behind the upright spar, down in front of the horizontal one, and then around behind the upright spar, passing just above the clove hitch made at the start. This process is repeated four times, keeping outside the earlier turns on the horizontal spar and inside them on the upright spar. This lashing is finished by taking three or four tight frapping turns around the turns binding the two spars together, and ending with a clove hitch on the horizontal spar, close to the lashing. This lashing, like most of the others, can be snugged by beating it with a short, heavy stick or the back of a light ax blade.

Diagonal Lashing

Diagonal lashings start with a timber hitch around both spars. This hitch is tightened to pull the two spars as close together as possible. Three or four turns of the rope are then taken entirely around one fork, where the spars touch, as in Figure 1, and then three or four turns are made entirely around the other fork. Two frapping turns are then tightly made between the two spars at the point where they cross, as in Figure 2, seizing the turns which hold the poles together. The lashing is finished with a clove hitch around the spar that is most convenient for the rope end which completes the frapping.

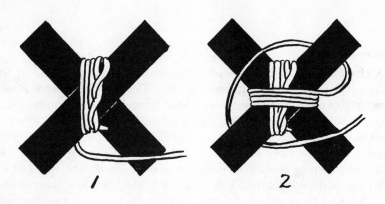

Shear Lashing

This lashing begins with a clove hitch on one of the two vertical spars and the turn taken around both parallel spars begins just under the clove hitch. When six or eight turns have been made around the two spars, the lashing ends with a tight frapping between the two spars, around the turns which bind them together, the end of the rope being tied with two half hitches, pulled very tight, at the foot of the lashing, on the spar opposite the starting clove hitch.

Tripod Lashing

To lash three spars together to form a tripod it is easiest to work with the spars on the ground. Place the spars as shown in the drawing and begin the lashing with a clove hitch, or timber hitch, on one of the outside spars. Make six or seven lashing turns, rather loosely, around the three spars and then two or three loose frapping turns between each of the two outside spars and the center one. End the frapping with a clove hitch on the center spar. This tripod will stand firmly when the three legs are spread out in position.

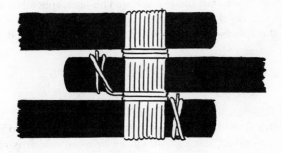

Marling

This useful hitch, also known as the hammock hitch and marline hitch, consists of a number of overhand knots made around an object, such as a hammock, tent, sail, or squares of canvas.

Tying. The "marling down" or lashing should be done with a length of light rope. Make a series of overhand knots, as shown in the drawing. To make this hitch correctly, the marling end (which runs the long way) must come out from the *under* side of the crossing.

SPLICING

Splicing well is a seagoing science, but everyday splicing can be done neatly and without much difficulty by the average knot tyer who is accustomed to work with ropes. A standard three-strand Manila rope is a good one on which to start the art of splicing. The only tools required, apart from the inevitable sailor knife, is a marlinspike, made of steel and tapering from the ¾- or 1-inch butt to a point, and a wooden fid, of hickory or other very hard wood, very similar in shape and length to the marlinspike. Both these tools are used to unlay rope and tuck ends under as one splices. There are many splices of different sorts, but three basic splices are all that the amateur seagoer need know. These are the short splice, the long splice, and the eye splice. The back splice has its uses, but a neat whipping on the end of the rope serves equally well and proves easier than the splicing method, which is frequently finished by an end-whipping.

Short Splice

A short splice is used to join two ropes which do not have to run through a pulley of the correct size or through an opening which is only slightly larger than the rope.

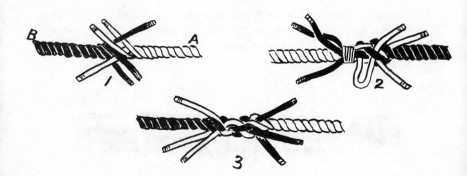

Splicing. Untwist the ends of each rope to be spliced, about five turns, depending on the size of the rope and how strong the splice needs to be. Place the two ropes together so that the strands alternate as in Figure 1.

The strands will stay neat more easily if you whip the end of each. To keep them out of the way, temporarily tie the three strands of rope B to rope A. Tuck one strand of rope A through the loop of rope B that is nearest to it, then do the same with the other two strands, as in Figure 2. Do the same thing with the strands of the other rope, once the tie has been removed, as in Figure 3. Continue tucking the ends under, alternating on one side of the splice, then the other, until each strand has been tucked under at least three times.

Cut off the ends of the strands *not too close to the rope.* For a tapered splice, cut off one third of the yarns from each strand; then take two more tucks with each strand. When the splicing is completed, roll and pound it on a hard surface with a mallet or the back of an ax blade.

Long Splice

The long splice is used to join two pieces of rope into one, which has to run through a pulley or through a block that offers very little clearance.

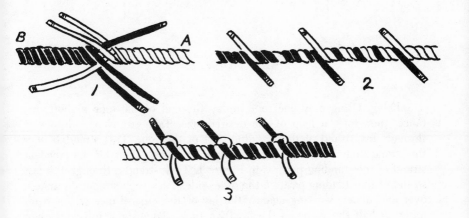

Splicing. Untwist the ends of the ropes about fifteen turns, about four times the length used for a short splice. Place the ropes together so that the strands alternate, as in Figure 1. Starting with any adjacent pair, unlay one strand and fill in with the strand from the other rope, as in Figure 2. Do the same thing with another pair of strands but, this time, work in the opposite direction. Leave the third pair where they are. As in Figure 3, tuck each strand down through the other, working with the lay of the rope. Tuck each twice, so that it continues going around the same strand. Reduce the number of yarns each time as you take two more tucks.

Cut off the strands close to the rope, and roll and pound the splice well.

Eye Splice

The eye splice is used in the end of a rope for mooring.

Splicing. Using only one rope, unlay the end of the rope a short distance, then form a loop of the desired size. Take strand a and tuck it through any strand of the standing part of the rope. Pass strand b *over* the strand under which strand a is tucked and pass it under the adjacent strand of the standing part, as in Figure 1. Tuck strand c through the last strand of the standing part, on the other side. Tuck each strand alternately over and under, working against the lay of the rope. Taper off by trimming off half the yarns on the last two tucks. Pound and roll well, then cut off the remaining strands close to the rope.

Grommets

Grommets are rope circles of varying size and thickness used for making handles for seagoing bags and chests, and they also serve for the game of quoits.

1   *2*   *3*

Tying. The length of the strand of rope to be used in making a grommet is decided by measuring the circumference of the grommet to be made and allowing three and one-half times this length.

Make an overhand knot in a piece of cord, then wind the cord back on itself, all the way around, forming a circle. This may be done two or three times, depending on the thickness of the grommet desired. Tie the two ends of the cord with a square knot.

One may also cover a metal ring with a string or cord, and larger grommets may be made with rope, splicing the ends and covering them evenly with string or cord.

A real sea-going grommet may be made with a length of Manila rope. Unlay one strand of the rope. Beginning at the center of the strand, twist one part around the other in the form of a circle, as in Figure 1. Continue to do this until a three-strand grommet is formed, as in Figure 3, and the ends of the strand meet. Tie the ends tightly with an overhand knot. Tuck the remaining ends under the other strands and trim off the remainder.

One can also make grommets by using the short splice method, but this is often not worth the time involved.

Putting Knots
and Ropes to Work

Knots and ropes have many uses apart from tying up a boat, putting up a tent, mountaineering, and other outdoor activities. Ropes, cords, and knots are useful for many things indoors too, such as these which follow.

ROPE HOUSE-PLATES

In the country and at the seaside, appropriate signs can be made with rope which give the name of either the house or its occupants. The oblong or oval plate which forms the background can be made of plywood or other wood, painted navy blue or white; the name on it formed by rope letters, the rope being dyed, or left white, to contrast with the background used. A coat of colorless varnish will keep the rope clean and weather-resistant. The thickness of the rope will determine the size of the plate and the visibility of the sign. The rope is nailed in the letter formation desired, using long, thin nails that have small heads, which go through the rope and enter firmly into the board. The illustration shows how such a nameplate is made. Those with an artistic bent may form the letters to look like longhand. It is wise to draw the outlines of the letters on the board in pencil before attaching them. An oval or oblong of rope may be used to encircle the letters.

KNOT TROPHY-PLAQUES

A knot tyer may have tied some beautiful or intricate knots which he may well wish to display as decoration. A good way to do so is to make the knots, bends, or hitches in heavy sash cord of the color desired, varnish them with colorless varnish, and then glue them onto an oval, oblong, or round plaque, of a color that will exhibit the knots to best advantage. Good quality rope, of varying thicknesses, may also be used in making the knots, and it may be dyed or left its natural color. The knots may be enclosed in a circle, oval, or oblong of heavy rope, glued or nailed onto the plaque, if desired.

CORK IN A BOTTLE

Uncorking a bottle is an easy job, done with a corkscrew, when the cork is in its proper place, but it is quite another thing when the cork has been pushed into the bottle and floats on top of the liquid. This situation can be taken care of easily. The first thing to do is to pour the contents of the bottle into a clean receptacle. Tie two or three knots, together, on the end of a piece of strong, heavy string. Push the knotted end of the string into the bottle so that it reaches just below the beginning of the bottle neck. Tilt the bottle so that the cork slides down the neck toward its mouth. Gently pull the string up into the neck of the bottle so that the cork in the neck is caught at its lower end by the knot. With an easy pull on the string, the cork will be pulled along with it out of the bottle, so that the liquid may be poured back and a new cork substituted for the old. The drawing shows better than words just how the cork may be removed.

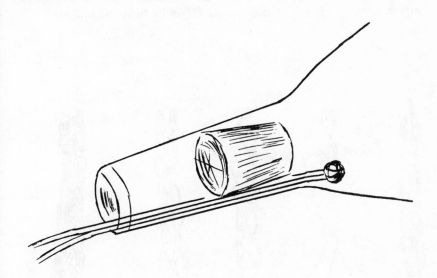

LANYARDS

There are literally dozens of weaves and braids, of varying thicknesses, used for making lanyards. Lanyards prove handy to fasten to watches, compasses, knives, whistles, and other similar objects, and so all outdoorsmen should be able to braid a simple lanyard, similar to the ones described below.

One-Strand Lanyard

This is a simple chain knot formed to the desired length, as in Figure 1.

Three-Strand Lanyard

This lanyard, made of three strands of light cord, is braided, one strand over the other, once the strands have been securely fastened at one end, as in Figure 2.

Four-Strand Lanyard

The lanyard in Figure 3 is two strands doubled back on themselves; and in Figure 4 the four strands are paired off by twos and braided.

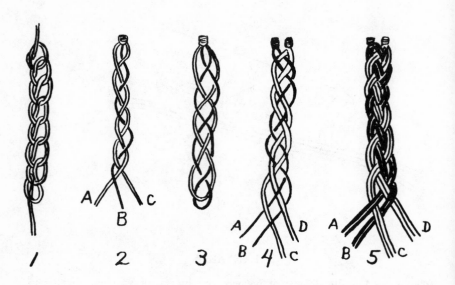

Four-Strand Lanyard Doubled

This lanyard is braided in the same way as the one in Figure 4, but the strands are braided in pairs, as illustrated in Figure 5.

There are many variations of these basic types of lanyards, with two, three, or more strands being used together and braided with other strands of equal size. Even the single chain may be used with two or three cords.

Lanyards can be made of a single color or two more colors, depending on the imagination of the weaver.

STRING AND KNOT CHARTS

Though many of the natives on remote islands in the Pacific have never seen a real chart, they navigate by the aid of effective charts of string, woven from various fibers, tied onto frames made of branches. They criss-cross the string on the frame, as shown in the drawing, and then seafaring natives who know the waters tie knots of varying sizes onto the crossed cords, to indicate the islands among which they are going to navigate in their native boats. Island chains, islets, and larger islands are indicated, in their approximate positions, by knots of different sizes. Though the natives use their own scale of measurements, the islands are placed with surprising accuracy, when compared with an actual chart, and these sea-farers know just how long it will take them to reach the various landfalls indicated on their string charts.

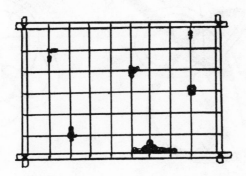

ROPE BUTTONS

There are many hard-to-make decorative buttons, and even "simple" buttons made from cord or rope are generally complicated affairs, being built on an inverted wall knot.

The simplest, most practical form of outdoors emergency button, made from cord or light rope, is formed by tying one or two square knots one on top of another, topped with a tightly tied overhand knot. Link buttons of this sort can be made by tying the knots mentioned above, at each end of a short length of heavy cord, leaving about three or four inches of cord between the buttons. These buttons are passed through cord loops, toggle style, sewn one on each side of a coat which has lost its buttons.

Ornamental Button

This ornamental button or cuff link design is a little more complicated than the one above, but very attractive.

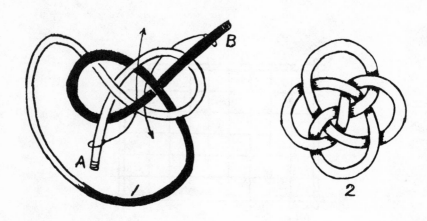

Form an underhand loop in the left hand with end A. Bring end B *under* the bight, *over* the standing part, *under* end A, *over* A's bight, and *under* its own standing part, as in Figure 1. Place the cord on a flat surface and, as indicated by the arrows, bring end A through *between* its bight and B's, then *over* its bight, on the other side. Then bring end B *under* A's bight, *under* its own bight, on the far side, and *over* its bight and A's bight on the near side, following the arrow. Turn the cord over and adjust the position of the loops. It may be used as a flat decoration, as in Figure 2. To make it into a knot, the loops must be worked into a tight button formation by pulling on the loops and the ends.

NECKERCHIEF TIE

This is the hitch that Navy men and Scouts use to tie their neckerchiefs. As will be seen in the drawing, it is made by tying a clove hitch in the standing part of the neckerchief.

ROPE LADDERS

A rope ladder is a handy thing aboard ship, in camp, or for general out-door use. There are a number of ways of making ladders from rope, or by a combination of rope, wooden rungs, or chocks. An all-rope ladder is useful and takes up very little room, and a combination rope and rung ladder has also many uses. Many rope ladders are made of rope thick enough to allow the wooden rungs to be pushed through the rope, after it has been opened with a fid. Since this type of ladder requires a 7- or 8-turn whipping, above and below the rung, seizing the rope on each side of the rung, two easier methods of making such a rung ladder are given here instead.

Double Rope and Rung Ladder

A strong, long-wearing ladder can be made by using two tough ropes of the same thickness, with strong, 12-inch-long wooden or lightweight metal rungs firmly lashed in place 12 inches apart, as in Figure 1. The rungs can also be held in place by being seized above and below by strong cord, the seizing beginning with a clove hitch, around both ropes, above each rung. The ropes should be pulled taut, from time to time, as the ladder making progresses, so that the rungs hang evenly. The length of the ladder is based, of course, on the double length of rope used on each side.

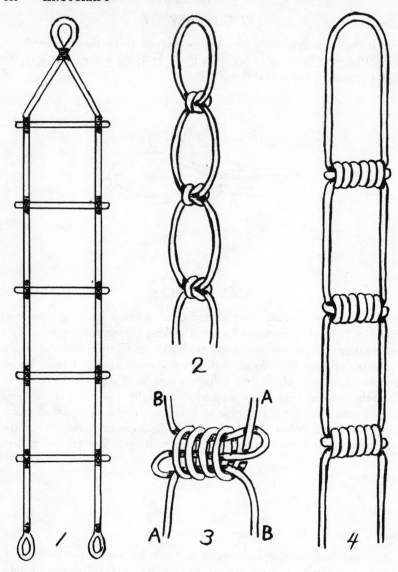

Single Rope and Rung Ladder

A more improvised form of rope ladder can be made by using a single strong rope on each side of the ladder, the rungs being securely bound to each side. Tying an overhand knot in the rope at each side at 12-inch intervals, to which the rungs can more easily be lashed, will assure their remaining in place despite wear and tear. This type of ladder requires much less rope than the one above.

Loop Ladder

This is an easily stowed, loop type of ladder. The loops may be joined by a square knot or blood knot, the latter being more difficult to tie. Make a bight at the center of the rope to hang the ladder up by, then make a square knot for each rung, as in Figure 2. The rungs should be about 12 to 14 inches apart.

All-Rope Ladder

Another easy-to-stow ladder can be made entirely out of stout rope by using the ladder rung knot, shown in Figure 3. Make a bight at the center of the rope, to hang it up by, then make a bight in rope B (as when preparing to make a sheepshank) about 12 to 14 inches from the top. Pass end A down through the bight at the right, take from 4 to 8 turns completely around the loops, then pass end A down through the bight at the left. Pull taut.

About 12 to 14 inches lower down, make a bight in rope A (in the opposite direction) and pass end B down through the bight at the left, take 4 to 8 turns completely around the loops, and pass end B down through the bight at the right. Pull taut.

Adjust the rope as you progress, so that the rungs will be even; and always make the same number of turns on each rung. Continue in this way, making the turns from right to left on rungs 1, 3, and 5 and from left to right on rungs 2, 4, and 6, until the ladder is the desired length.

RAPPELLING

Rappelling is the way to brake yourself up or down a steep slope or cliff by means of a single or double length of stout rope. The drawing shows just how one rappels. For a descent, the rope is passed around a tree or solid stump or a rock, at the top of the cliff or bank. Then the double rope goes around one thigh, upward across the chest, over the shoulder, then down across the back. The rope is grasped firmly by one hand while the other hand holds the rope on the opposite side of the body from the rope-encircled thigh. The body should be held in line with the cliff, the feet should be spread apart and pressed against projections on the cliff face, whenever the chance arises. In this way, the climber eases down the cliff face by slightly relaxing the grip on the ropes with the hands. The rate of descent can be slowed and completely checked at will by simply tightening the grip on the rope. Heavy clothing should be worn or soft sacks can be used as padding where the rope presses most on the body, at the shoulders, back, and thigh, as a protection against chafing and possible rope burns. All rope used for climbing should be tested and strong enough to stand any strain which may be put on it. (See "Choosing Rope," in Chapter 2.)

A handy feature of rappelling with a double rope is that one can pull the rope clear of the tree or stump when one reaches the foot of the cliff by merely pulling on one end of the rope, provided one does not wish to use it for a climb back to the top of the cliff again. A heavy single rope about 1 inch in diameter can be used for rappelling in the case where the rope is left in a fixed place for some time and does not need to be pulled down after the last climber has made the descent.

When several climbers are at the foot of a cliff and an ascent has to be

made, it is the job of someone who has some skill in climbing, to be the first to climb the cliff and attach the rope securely for the others who follow.

Though the once hard and fast precept, "Never climb up what you can't climb down" has been modified to some extent by rappelling, it is still a sound rule.

HEAVING LINE (Lifesaving)

There are several ways of making heaving lines, which are not related to the heaving line used for carrying a hawser out to a ship or onto a dock. The easiest way to make a heaving line for lifesaving purposes—man overboard, for example—is to fill a small canvas bag with about 1½ pounds of sand. Seize it to the end of a strong, light line, about 125 feet long. This line should be kept dry until put into use and used for no purpose other than lifesaving. Such a line is effective and does away with the need for difficult knots, such as the monkey's fist.

Practice and friendly contests in the use of the heaving may pay off. The target may consist of a wooden hoop about 18 inches in diameter, and the competitions can be carried out by throwing the lifeline at distances ranging from 50 to 100 feet.

TOURNIQUET (First Aid)

Before describing this knot, the authors wish to point out that a tourniquet of any sort is a *very dangerous* thing. Even in the case of a venomous snakebite or a fairly severe hemorrhage, the use of a tourniquet to stop temporarily the flow of blood should be employed with extreme caution. A piece of thin rubber tubing or a handkerchief makes a safer tourniquet than a piece of soft rope. The piece of rubber tubing or handkerchief is wrapped around the injured part, above or below the wound, depending on whether the hemorrhage is arterial or venous, and the two ends tied with a square knot. The drawing shows how the short stick which tightens the tourniquet is inserted. When no stick can speedily be found, a second square knot is tied an inch or two above the first one and used as a means of twisting the tourniquet tight.

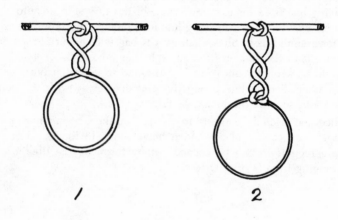

1   2

RAFT BUILDING

Good rafts can be made without too much difficulty by using a few dry, buoyant logs, preferably of pine, balsam, or fir, sawed from the butts of *dead* trees, and a few lengths of heavy cord or light rope, provided the would-be raft builders know how to tie knots and one or two simple lashings. How to tie knots and lash is told elsewhere in this book. A catamaran raft is easier to build than an oblong one, requires much less material, and is seaworthy, so it is the raft described here.

When one builds a raft for the first time, it is always surprising to discover how many suitable logs are required to support even *one* person. The size of the raft will be decided by the logs available, but they should be as large and buoyant as possible because it takes a lot of floating material to support the weight of the rafters who hope to ride on it.

The catamaran raft floats more easily than a square or oblong one because the feet and legs of the rafters riding it are in the water. The drawing shows a raft of this sort. The rafters sit astride the center log. The narrow plank in the center of the raft carries the gear. The two outside, smaller logs are the outriggers, balance logs, on which nobody rides. When raft builders are novice knot tyers, notches can be cut in the logs to make certain that lashings do not slip. Cords or ropes which have been dipped in oil of some sort will withstand the water and weather better than untreated rope.

Only those who swim reasonably well should ride on any raft, unless the craft is well made and has at least one good swimmer aboard.

TRACKING A CANOE OR SMALL BOAT°

This method of leading small craft, from dry land, by walking along a lakeshore or the bank of a stream or river, is also known as lining. This is how it is done. Two tracking lines are required. They should be about 50 feet long for all-purpose tracking, though they can be considerably shorter when tracking conditions are favorable. These lines can be either thin, strong rope or heavy sash cord. One end of these cords is fastened to the bow and the other to the stern of the craft, as far forward and aft as it is possible to fasten firmly the ends of the lines to the gunwales or other convenient points.

It is interesting and, at first, surprising as one practices this art along the treeless shoreline of a lake, to see that the canoe runs forward on its own accord and that it can easily be headed out from or toward shore by simple manipulation of the lines. A slight pull on the bow line or a little tug on the stern line does the trick. When the shoreline is sandy and the

° From *Living Like Indians*, by Allan A. Macfarlan (New York: Association Press, 1961).

water shallow enough for wading, it is pleasant in summer to wade along with the boat performing alongside in deeper water.

When one has mastered the easy art of tracking a boat or canoe along a lakeshore, it is time to try tracking along the bank of a slow-flowing river. Of course, the banks of a stream which is comparatively free from trees and tall rocks close to the water's edge make for ideal tracking. Two men can track a canoe, instead of one, with one man on the bow line and the other handling the stern line, but it is surprising how easily the work can be done single-handed.

At times, the authors had to use ropes even longer than 50 feet in order to have enough spare line to guide canoes around rocks cropping up some distance from shore, in cases where the canoe had to be tracked around the outside of such rocks rather than on the shoreward side. Tracking can be done either from the same level as the canoe or from the bank of a stream considerably higher than the stream. A slight pull on one line while letting out the other, works wonders for steering the obedient craft around obstacles.

ROPE TENT-FRAMES

Rope can be used easily and efficiently as frames for certain tents, improvised tents, and shelters. This method makes it unnecessary to use regular poles or to improvise poles by cutting saplings on the campsite. Heavy cord or strong, lightweight rope makes excellent frameworks on which to stretch the fabrics for improvised tents. The drawings show how the ropes can be stretched between convenient trees or poles in order to form the tent-frames.

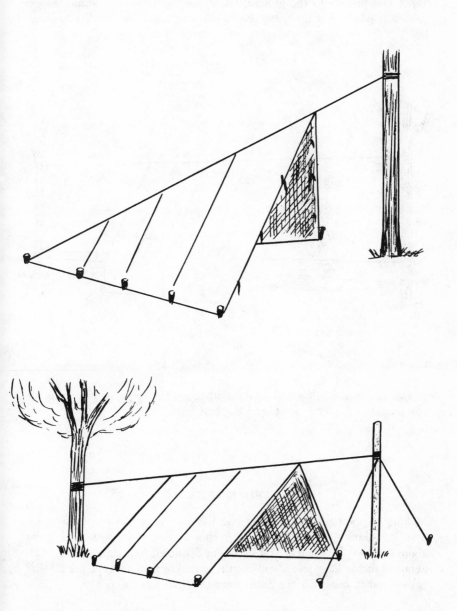

An improvised wedge tent, slung between two trees, as shown, can be made into a wall tent with walls about 2 feet high, by simply lashing a crosspiece, the width of the front of the tent, firmly onto each of the two trees, at the height desired, and tying a length of rope from each end of one pole to the other pole. The fabric is draped over these wall-forming ropes and pegged to the ground. Of course, walls always require longer pieces of fabric, but the extra comfort is well worth the small extra cost.

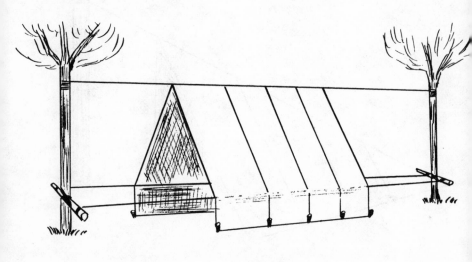

The principal hitches and knots used to tie the ropes in place are the clove hitch, the square knot, and the half hitch.

ROPE BEDS

Making a rope bed is easy when one has learned a few simple lashings. Two logs about 3½ feet long and 6 inches in diameter, two smooth poles about 7½ feet long and 3 or 4 inches in diameter, four stout stakes, each about 12 inches long, and a few lengths of thin or medium rope are all that is required to construct the entire framework of this camp bed.

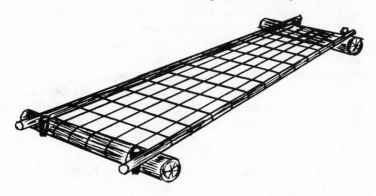

The drawing shows how the logs, poles, stakes, and rope are arranged. The two poles are lashed, 2½ or 3 feet apart, to the logs with diagonal lashings, at each end, *or* the poles may be held in place without lashing, the stakes keeping them in place. The rope is wound across the poles, from side to side, the strands being from 4 to 6 inches apart, and from head to foot of the framework in the same way. Of course, the closer the strands, the more comfortable the bed. To hold the rope in place, shallow notches can be cut at the outside of each pole or every second or third turn may be secured to the poles by a clove hitch. The same method may be used to attach the rope to the head and foot logs, each rope being passed around the log and secured with a clove hitch.

Such a bed, when covered with a blanket or two, is cool and comfortable, and the framework is equally useful to support a sleeping bag. The length of time the bed is to be used will decide just how firmly the framework should be lashed and the ropes tied in position.

The ropes may be covered with a piece of heavy canvas 40 inches wider than the bed, to allow 20 inches on each side to pass around the pole and be sewn just inside the pole, along the entire length of the bed.

BUNKS

A serviceable, inexpensive bunk for a summer cabin can be made by constructing a light, strong plank framework about 6 feet long by 2½ feet wide. The planks may be 6 to 8 inches wide by 1 inch thick. When using the above measurements, mark each plank about 3 inches from the top edge and along its entire length with crayon or pencil, each mark indicating where a small hole is to be drilled. The marks should be 6 inches apart and 3 inches from each end of the long planks, and 5 inches apart and 2½ inches from each end of the short planks. At each pencil mark, drill a small hole about ½ inch in diameter, or slightly larger than the rope to be passed through it.

Starting at one end, make a stopper knot, then weave the rope back and forth, through the holes, the length and width of the bed, as illustrated. Fasten the rope securely at the end with another stopper knot. Stout legs of the desired length may be screwed to the four corners of the bunk.

If different measurements are used, the holes may be spaced from 4 to 6 inches apart, as desired.

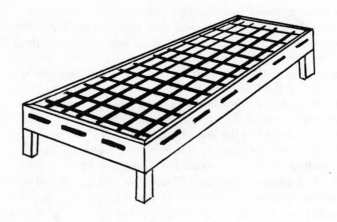

LOG ROLLING

A parbuckle is useful for rolling logs and other cylindrical objects on land and works well on fairly smooth terrain free from rocks and tree stumps. A similar device, using pulleys, is used to hoist heavy masts and spars on board ship.

The only gear required is a length of stout rope ½ to ¾ inch in diameter and from 20 to 30 feet long, and a stout stake about 12 inches long and 2½ inches in diameter, tapering to a point.

The stake is driven into the ground at a fairly acute angle, slanting away from the log, and from 6 to 10 feet away from it. The center of the rope is placed around the stake, as shown in the drawing, and the two ends taken to the log. One end of the log is raised slightly. One end of the rope is slipped under it and then around, behind, and over the top of the log. The same thing is done at the other end of the log. With one or two persons pulling gently on the ends of the rope, the log will roll easily toward the stake. When the log reaches the stake, the stake is pulled out and driven in again about 8 feet away. The rope is then adjusted as before, and the log rolled on the next leg of its course.

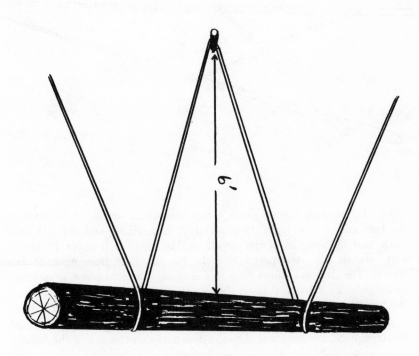

MAKING A TRAVOIS

The travois shown in the drawing was used by the Indians as a means of transporting tepees and baggage of all sorts. Sometimes a small travois was pulled by a dog, harnessed between the poles of the framework, and the big travois was pulled by a horse, hitched between the two poles, at the narrow end. Quite often, squaws pulled such travois as they glided along smoothly, in suitable country, and kept baggage from touching the damp ground. Travois are still useful in camp. Building the framework affords an opportunity for making diagonal hitches, and tying the bundle in place on the crosspiece calls for ability to tie either the diamond hitch or the squaw hitch. The travois, therefore, finds a place in this book.

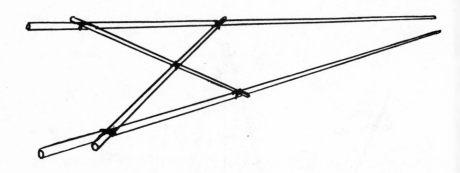

Two light, straight poles about 6 feet long and 2 inches in diameter at the butt end, two straight sticks about 30 inches long and about 1 inch thick, and five lengths of thick cord or thin rope, each about 18 inches long, are all that is required to make the complete framework of one travois. The diagram shows how this is done. The crosspiece is fastened to the poles by a diagonal lashing at each end of the sticks; and, if desired, the two sticks may be joined where they cross by another diagonal lashing.

An additional length of light rope is required to hitch the bundle onto the crosspiece, the length of the rope depending on the size of the bundle.

An interesting and amusing speed contest in tying lashings, necessary for building the travois, is given in Chapter 7 under "Travois Race."

6

Games With Rope

This chapter of rope-fun games has been included to supply entertainment while showing how to tie knots. All the games may be played by young and old: all require ropes. The term "leader," used throughout this chapter, is to designate any adult who volunteers, or is chosen, to lead a game. Practically any grown-up can do so successfully.

A number of the games which follow require self-control, patience, quick action, coordination, and, in the team games, cooperation. Most of the games require almost no equipment, except for some rope or cord, and they have been written in an easy-to-follow fashion so that no trouble will be experienced in staging them.

Written or adapted especially for this book, the games add up to FUN while helping to develop camaraderie and good sportsmanship.

LET'S PLAY!

ROPE SNATCH

In this challenge game, a player called the guardian kneels or sits cross-legged in the center of a circle, 10 feet in diameter, marked on the ground or floor. A small circle, 2 feet in diameter, is marked directly in the center of the large circle. Four short lengths of stout rope, each 8 inches long, are placed in the form of a square around the central player. One end of each

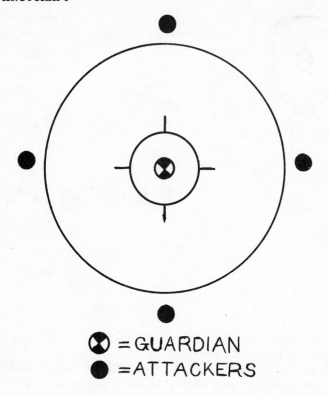

⊗ = GUARDIAN

● = ATTACKERS

rope length touches the edge of the small circle and the other points directly outward, like the spokes of a wheel.

The job of the player in the center is to guard the rope lengths from four attackers, one on each side of the outer circle, at the start of the game. When the leader calls "Go!" the attackers advance to try to secure a rope. Each attacker may get only one rope at a time and must place a rope he has successfully snatched on the floor outside the large circle before he can return for another piece of rope.

The guardian puts an attacker out of the game by striking him on the hand as he reaches for a rope end. The guardian may use his hand to strike the attackers, or the leader may give him a switch made of three 12-inch lengths of soft cotton rope, whipped together at one end. Any attacker touched by hand or whip is out of the game and retires outside the big circle. The rope remains in place.

Played at its best, this game is not a mere grab and run event, since each attacker should approach slowly and deceive the guardian by feinting, before trying to seize one of the rope ends. The player who captures the greatest number of rope ends without being touched is the winner.

Leaders can devise variations of this game by using six rope ends, instead of four, having two attackers instead of four, or deciding that attackers may snatch only with the left hand, for instance.

ROPE WALK

This game is based on the time when the rope maker used to walk backward, in a long, straight line, paying out fiber from the coil around his waist as he went. The only equipment required for this game is a starting line marked on the floor or ground, and another line 20 or 30 feet distant and directly opposite. These two lines are connected at 3- or 4-foot intervals by heavy chalk lines, representing the rope walks (instead of chalk lines, binder cord or cheap, heavy string can be used).

There are two players to each rope walk. One is the weaver and the other is his helper, and it is difficult to say which has the harder job. At the start of each race, the weaver and his helper form a team of two and stand together at the starting line, directly beside a rope-walk line.

On the word "Go!" from the leader of the game, the weaver starts down the line, backward, trying to walk *directly* on the line, his helper walking just behind him, in order to direct and encourage him to keep to the straight and narrow path. At the second line, they turn about by the left and, still walking backward, return to the starting point, which becomes the finish line. To make things a little harder for the weaver, from start to finish, he has to pantomime paying out rope from around his waist, as he walks backward. The weaver may look back over his shoulder at any time, but a good helper should make this unnecessary and save the team valuable time.

In order to demonstrate to the weaver that the helper's lot is not a happy one, he may change places for a second race. The former helper then becomes the weaver. Each rope-walk team competes against the others and the first team to finish, which has held well to the line, is the winner.

This race may also be contested by one player, instead of partners; in this form of the race, he has to do his own helping and, above all, keep on the line, in addition to walking as quickly as the situation will allow.

This is an amusing game for the onlookers, and the majority of them —whether there is an official helper or not—usually offer advice of a more or less helpful nature.

RING IN A RING

This game is an adaptation of one played by the American Indians of the Southwest. They used rings made from flexible twigs, but knot-tying people who have spare rope ends or ready-made grommets have the necessary equipment at least half made. Two grommets, one measuring 3½ inches in diameter and the other 2¾ inches in diameter, are the only equipment required for the game.

The big ring was placed flat on the ground; and the Indians, from a distance of 10 to 20 feet, tried to toss the smaller ring into the big ring, so that it stayed inside. The winner was sometimes decided by the best score in three or six throws, but often the game was played for a long time, the winner being decided as the result of many throws.

It will be seen that the size of the rings used by the Indians did not allow much leeway; so the leader may decide to use a smaller ring, around 2 inches in diameter, leaving the size of the larger ring unchanged. Of course, the idea for this game is the chief thing, and a leader may decide to play it with rings which are considerably larger, the larger one being about 6 inches in diameter and the smaller about 4½ or 5 inches. Rope rings, such as those used for the game of quoits may be used, or grommets, made by the knot tyers, are also good for Ring in a Ring.

A few rope rings can be especially spliced for this game. It saves time if a player stands beside the target ring and retrieves the small ring for the players.

ON TARGET!

This game requires a round target made from stout, white cardboard. It is 36 inches in diameter, marked with a black bull's-eye 2 inches in diameter. A 5-inch circle, then a 1-inch marker-circle, another 5-inch circle and a 1-inch marker-circle, and finally a 5-inch circle surround the bull's-eye. The inner 1-inch circle should be painted red, and the outer one yellow. Three rope grommets, one 6 inches in diameter and two 4 inches in diameter, made from ¾-inch rope, and one 2-foot length of ½-inch dowel stick complete the play gear.

A throwing line is marked on the floor about 20 feet away from the target and directly opposite it. The players take turns at throwing all three grommets, one at a time, from just behind the throwing line.

A grommet touching any part of the bull's-eye counts 10 points; touching the area between the bull's-eye and including the red marker-circle counts 6; touching the area up to and including the yellow marker-circle counts 4; and the area from the edge of the target to the yellow line counts 2.

The catch in this stunt is that the grommets have to be thrown from the end of the dowel throwing-stick. This is considerably more difficult than throwing the rings by hand, but it is more fun.

As a variation, or when this game is played by younger players, the throwing may be done by hand, using the same method of scoring.

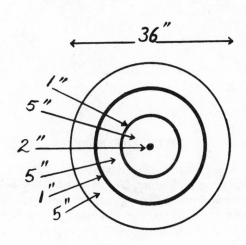

GIVE-AWAY GAME°

This game is based on the giving-of-gifts ceremony held by Indian chiefs in honor of special achievements of their sons. It is a "scramble" game, and leaders should see that it is not played with too great enthusiasm. The fact that it is played in a small circle makes it a safe game for all age groups. The Indian game, played in a big circle, was the cause of a number of good-humored collisions.

The guests (players) generally stood in a huge circle, facing outward, while the chief, usually a member or relative of the family sponsoring the celebration, stood just outside the ring of guests. At intervals, feinting as he threw, he tossed small sticks, about 4 inches long and ½ inch thick,

---

° See *Living Like Indians*, by Allan A. Macfarlan (New York: Association Press, 1961).

into various parts of the circle. Each stick represented a horse or a fine blanket; and the first person to run from his place in the circle and snatch up the stick, in the face of strong competition, and only *after* it first hit the ground, could collect the prize.

Today, the game may be played by using a circle about 30 feet in diameter; and the sticks may be replaced by a dozen 4-inch lengths of rope, ranging in size from ½ inch to 1 inch in diameter. If the ends are nicely whipped, these "sticks" will be good for many games.

This is a good game with which to teach younger Space-Age braves to be on the alert and, of course, the game may be played without giving the winners either horses or blankets.

OVER THE ROPE

The easiest and safest way to play this game is for two players to be seated on chairs, facing each other, 20 feet apart. They hold a length of ½-inch rope between them, at varying heights, starting at about 12 inches from the floor and gradually moving it upward, a few inches at a time, until a height is reached which no player can step over or negotiate by a standing jump.

The players all approach the rope from the same side and after stepping over it successfully, circle around to the starting side for another try at a higher level. The leader of the game, assisted by the two rope holders, rules out any player who touches the rope with any part of his feet or body, in trying to step over it. Players ruled out retire from the play area.

The two players manipulating the rope try to keep it at an even level along it entire length. They should be ready to let at least one end go, should a player catch his foot on it in trying to cross the rope by a standing jump, provided the leader allows this method of getting across.

Some knot-tying groups who have taken up this game seriously either have a thin pole, marked in feet and inches, lashed to each chair so that the rope holders can regulate the heights at which they hold the rope, or, in some cases, have two poles, supported on a heavy stand, with pegs driven into them at certain distances, supporting a light pole instead of a rope. The pegs face away from the approaching players, of course. This gear may be worth the trouble taken to make it, when it is used for this game and the one which follows.

UNDER THE ROPE

This game is based on the Limbo game of the West Indies. It may be played, with the same equipment, in exactly the opposite way from the preceding game, except that the rope manipulators start at an easy height of about 5 feet and gradually lower the rope to a foot or so from the floor. Instead of going over the rope, the players duck under it. Of course, this becomes more and more difficult as the rope is held lower and lower. No player may lie on the floor in order to get under, and any player who touches the rope with any part of his body or touches the floor with hands or body is ruled out of the game.

Under the Rope provides good exercise, and it is surprising how close some supple players can pass between the rope and floor without touching either rope or floor with their bodies.

FOUR-ROPE GUESSING GAME

This is one of the most interesting of the hundreds of guessing games played by the Indians throughout the Americas. The Chinook Indians of the Northwest Coast played the game with four rounded hardwood sticks 12 inches long. Two of these sticks, which were beautifully decorated, were 1 inch in diameter and the other two were ½ inch in diameter. The Indian Cliff Dwellers of Arizona played the game with sticks 7 inches long.

As knot tyers, we may use four rope ends, whipped to prevent fraying; two ropes are 8 inches long and 1 inch in diameter, and the other two, the same length but only ½ inch in diameter. A circular piece of cloth about 18 inches in diameter is also needed.

One player challenges another, and they sit on the floor or ground facing each other. One arranges the rope ends under the cloth in any of the six ways shown in the drawing, and his opponent guesses the arrangement. Players take turns arranging and guessing, the player who guesses correctly continuing to do so until he guesses wrongly; then the other player does the guessing. The players (or a leader) keep score, and the winner is the one who guesses correctly most often in three or six games.

Should this game prove too difficult for the players, the leader may limit the positions in which the rope ends may be placed from six to only three or four.

CHIPPEWA GUESSING GAME

The Indians played this game with slim sticks or reeds, but, true to the tradition of ropes, in this case it is played with short lengths of stiff rope or cord about ⅜ inch in diameter. There should be from fifteen to twenty-seven lengths, each about 3 inches long, for each two players. There must always be an odd number of rope lengths. Whipping the ends will assure their long life for future games.

Two players contest, and there may be as many couples contesting as there are pieces of rope required for each two players. One player takes the bundle of rope ends in both hands and divides the bundle into two handfuls of about equal size. Neither player should be able actually to count the rope ends. He extends both closed hands, backs upward, each containing a bundle of cords. His opponent then quickly chooses either of the bundles, then each player counts the number of cords which his bundle holds. The player with an even number of cords wins 1 point toward the game's total score, which can range from 6 to 30.

The winner of the first round continues to present the cords as long as he continues getting an even number. When he fails to do so, his opponent takes the entire bundle and does the dividing and presenting of the cords, until he fails to get an even number; then he returns them to the first player.

FENCE TAG

The only things required for this game are about 30 feet of lightweight, soft string which will break easily, and two chairs or stools. The string is fastened to the legs of the two chairs, placed about 30 feet apart, so that the string is about 15 inches above the floor or ground level, along its entire length.

One player volunteers to be "It" and stands on one side of the string fence, while three to six players stand on the other side. The leader of the game calls "Go!" and the players may then jump over the string at any point between the chairs. They run the risk of being tagged by "It," who may tag only those who come over onto his side of the fence.

All players tagged drop out of the game, and the leader may rule out any one or two of the last untagged players because they do not dare to take chances on the "dangerous" side of the fence.

When the string is broken, it should be joined again before the game continues. The leader should choose a new "It" for each game and, if he likes, appoint a second "It" in case the first has too much difficulty in tagging the other players.

RACE ON PLACE

This "race" provides exercise for the participants and amusement for the onlookers. A 56-inch length of light rope or cord is required for each contestant, and there should be three or four players competing.

The leader forms circles, which are approximately 18 inches in diameter, about 6 feet apart, with the coils of rope, one length to a circle with the ends meeting but not overlapping. A player stands in the center of each circle. He explains that each rope circle is supposed to be one foot high and that as the racers compete they must lift their feet at least 12 inches above the ground in order to be in the running. He also warns that the race will be judged not only on endurance but also by the style of the runners. He will tell them the number of steps which they are to run, *within the circle*, and each runner will count out the steps as they are run. This procedure does not make the race any easier for the contestants.

The leader calls "Ready!—one hundred steps—Run!" whereupon each runner immediately starts to race, lifting his feet high, and, if he likes, swinging his arms and counting each step out loud, to the confusion of his racing neighbors. The leader need not, up to a certain point, take the actual number of steps run too seriously. Once a player announces one hundred and stops running, the only things that count are whether he finishes first, second, or third and what his style was like throughout the race. If the style of a runner who finishes second is superior to that of the one who finishes first, the runner who came in second is declared the winner.

Any player who steps outside the circle—and it is no easy task to stay within its bounds—is ruled out of the game. Strangely enough, many runners cannot stay within the circle for more than twenty or thirty steps. Perhaps a sense of balance is lacking. The leader bases the number of steps to be run on the age and prejudged stamina of the runners. Two hundred and fifty steps will prove a long and tough race!

MOON FLIGHT

For this game construct a circle of stout cardboard, 18 inches in diameter, and paint it in show card colors to resemble the moon, as shown in the drawing. The area marked with a circle should be 6 inches in diameter. Three grommets made of stiff rope ½ to ¾ inches thick, each 4 inches in diameter, complete the gear needed.

The "moon" is laid on the floor, and a throwing line is marked directly opposite the moon and about 20 feet distant. The players take turns at throwing the three grommets, one at a time, in an attempt to make moon landings. Each successful landing scores 6 points. To make the landings a little more difficult, a forbidden zone is shown on the central, left-hand

side. No landing may be made on this area; spacecraft landing there will lose 5 points, and the astronaut who does so forfeits any of the remaining flights until his turn comes again.

The player who first makes a score of 18 or 36, as decided by the leader, is the winner. Of course, the throwing distance can be increased or shortened, based on the skill of the players.

STEPPING-STONES

The gear required for this game is six 46-inch lengths of light rope or cord. A chalk line is marked on the floor at the starting point, and another line is drawn directly opposite and about 30 feet distant.

Six players form three teams of two players in each. They stand, with 6 feet between teams, just behind the starting line. One player on each team is given two lengths of rope and is told that his job is to form two circles, each about 15 inches in diameter, by placing the ropes on the floor, so that the two ends of each rope meet. The player forming the circles must complete the circle before his partner can step or jump into it, as he races, from circle to circle, from the starting line to the opposite line and back again.

The player who places the circles must be careful to place them about 2 feet apart and form real circles with each rope, so that his partner will have room to stand with both feet inside each circle, just as soon as it has been formed. Immediately a player touches any part of a rope with any part of either foot, he is ruled out of the game and his team loses.

This game can be played quite cleverly. The success of the winning team is largely achieved by the speed and skill of the player who lays the stepping-stones. If he places them too close together, his team loses time, but if he places them too far apart, his teammate will either fail to land cleanly on a stone or will lose his balance and step off it, after making a clumsy landing. Of course, the player who steps or jumps from stone to stone is also a winning factor in the game. If he moves before the circle is completely formed, his team is disqualified; and if he loses his balance so that he steps, even for a second, off a stone, he loses the race for his team.

ISLAND HOP

The same gear is required for this game as for Stepping-stones. Each player contests against the others; they start by standing just behind a line marked on the floor, with 6 feet between players. The finish line, about 30 feet distant, is marked directly opposite.

On the word "Go!" each player forms a rope circle in front of him, fairly close to his feet, then jumps into it. While standing in the first circle, each player takes the second length of rope and forms a circle with it a few feet, not too far, ahead of him and jumps into it. The players continue this method of play, always reaching back for the circle just left and forming a new circle as speedily as possible, until they reach the finish line.

It will be seen that each circle must be formed in such a way that both feet may be placed inside it without touching the rope (because if a player's foot touches the rope or goes outside the rope ring he is disqualified and out of the game, as in Stepping-stones), and that the circles should not be formed too far apart or the players may fail to jump cleanly into them.

Some players make excellent time by speedy action in forming the circles, and this holds true even when they place the circles fairly close together.

The leader may ask older contestants to turn at the second line and race back to the starting line, where the race finishes. In either form, the first player to finish is the winner, providing he has made clean jumps.

FOUR-WAY TUG-OF-WAR

This is a tug-of-war which can be contested indoors by either girls or boys. The only gear needed is an 8-foot length of ¾-inch rope and four paper cups of identical size.

The four contestants hold the rope loosely and move around until it is held in the form of a square, with one tugger at each corner facing away from the center. Now, a paper cup is placed about 3 feet in front of each tugger. The judge or leader says "Take the strain," waits a moment to see that the players are correctly placed to form a square, then calls "Go!" Each player then tries to move steadily forward and pick up the cup directly in front of him. The first to do so is the winner. He falls out, another player takes his place, and the tug commences as before.

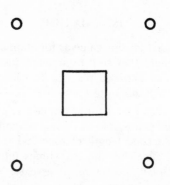

ROPE-HOLD TAG

This tag game is played best outdoors. The only gear required is a 6-foot length of ½-inch rope. There are two "Its" and each holds one *end* of the rope throughout the game. These two players chase and try to tag the other players, who should keep within certain bounds set by the leader.

The main difficulty for the taggers is that they must keep the rope taut, extended to its full 6 feet, while they pursue the other players. The "Its" may run side by side or one behind the other, either leading, and either may tag any player, *but* the tagging does not count unless the rope is kept taut.

The rope does not prove a big handicap because, quite frequently, players take chances which they would not take if they were being pursued by a single tagger. Leaders can experiment with ropes of different lengths when directing this game.

CROSS-STEP ROPE TUG

This is a balance race, made more difficult with the help of a rope. The only gear required is a 4-foot length of ½-inch rope for each two contestants. A straight line 30 feet long is marked on the floor or ground, for each player, and the lines are 3 feet apart. Each player holds a rope end in the hand nearer his rival.

When the leader calls "Go!" each player swings his right foot so that it crosses in front of the toes of the left foot, bringing the heel of the right foot against the outer side of the left foot, to a point about halfway between the heel and toe. The contestants must keep their feet pointing straight ahead as they advance. The left foot is swung alongside the right in the same manner, and this continues until the players reach the end of the line.

Since the contestant who *keeps* his balance is the likely winner, each tries to help the other *lose* his balance by occasional tugs on his end of the rope at unexpected moments.

Knotcraft Fun

This is a chapter of fun with knots and hitches, and all the games are entirely different from those in the preceding chapter. A number of the games call for the use of various skills associated with knotcraft. There are knot races, relays, and contests, interspersed with guessing games, stressing play in a lighter vein. Some games require varying skills in knot tying and dexterity. The adult who volunteers to lead some of these games should have a fairly good knowledge of knots and how to tie them, since in the few technical knotting games, knots must be examined for correctness in order to decide on the winning contestants.

KNOT-TYING CONTESTS: BLINDFOLD OR VISUAL

Exciting contests can be held among knot tyers of fairly equal skill, and often competitions between girls and boys of all ages prove the most exciting of all. The knots and hitches chosen for such contests should be six or eight of the simple basic knots and hitches, such as square, bowline, fisherman's, sheepshank, clove hitch, sheet bend, figure-of-eight, two half hitches, and timber hitch.

To be most effective, this contest should be held with not more than six knotters competing at the same time. Three boys and three girls may participate, either as individual contestants, or as two teams of three in each.

The only gear required for this event is a supply of sash cord, cut into 3-foot lengths, *two* cords for each knotter, and either a 12-inch length of 1-inch pole or ½ - to ¾ -inch dowel stick 12 inches long for each competitor.

The contests can be carried out with the eyes open or, for more advanced contestants, blindfolded. The name of the knot to be tied is announced by the judge, and each knotter starts tying the knot either on the blast of a whistle or on the word "Go!" Immediately a contestant has finished a knot, he throws it on a table before him or, if there is no table, he holds it above his head.

A judge (or judges) reads aloud the order in which the knotters finish; then the knots are carefully examined to be certain that they have been correctly tied. If the competitors are blindfolded, they may be allowed to watch the judging of each knot, and are then blindfolded again, ready to tie the next knot.

The winner is the contestant who correctly ties the most knots out of six, eight, or more, the fastest. Such an event provides fun and training for players of all ages.

SIX-KNOT RACE

The gear required for this race is one 3-foot length of sash cord for each contestant. The players stand 3 feet apart just behind a chalk line marked on the floor or ground. Opposite each contestant and about 30 feet distant is a small paper plate, on which one length of cord is placed.

On the word "Go!" each player races to the plate opposite him, and ties six overhand knots, about 3 inches apart, on the cord, trying to space the knots fairly evenly. This is not easy when one is in a hurry and has a competitor on each side trying to tie knots faster than he. Immediately a player has *finished* tying the sixth knot, and not before, he races back to the starting line holding his knotted cord above his head.

A leader notes the sequence of each player's arrival at the starting line, then compares the cords in order to see which player has done the neatest and most accurately spaced knotting job. The winner is the contestant who has made the fastest time, and at the same time has observed even spacing of his knots. In this contest, a player coming in second, but with a near-perfect knotting job, may be judged the winner.

KNOT RELAY

This little race requires self-control on the part of the players and causes amusement and excitement among the spectators.

The equipment required for twelve players is six small paper plates and three 3-foot lengths of sash cord. The three plates are placed 3 feet apart at one end of the room. The other three plates are placed directly in line, at the other end of the room, 20 or 30 feet away if space permits. One length of sash cord is coiled on each plate, opposite the starting line.

Three contesting teams of four runners each stand behind the three plates at the starting line. The leader explains that the first player is to run to the plate opposite, tie an overhand knot *snugly* but *not* tightly toward one end of the cord, replace the cord in a neat coil on the plate, then run back to touch off the second player on his team and fall in at the end of the line. The second player runs to the plate, unties the knot, coils the cord on the plate, touches off the third player, and falls in at the end of the line. The third player races to the plate and ties an overhand knot, as the first player did, coils the rope, and touches off the fourth before falling in. The fourth player races to the plate and unties the knot, coils the cord, and runs back to fall in at the end of the line.

A leader, or other player, stands behind the plates in which the cords are coiled to see that the cords have been knotted or unknotted and properly coiled as the race progresses. The first team to finish wins, provided the members have tied and untied the cord correctly and in proper sequence and replaced the cord, neatly coiled, in the plate after either tying or untying the knot. The leader of the game makes the decision regarding the winning team.

KNOT DETECTIVE

It may not seem difficult to detect a knot, but it is when the players are blindfolded and the identification is done by the fingers! This little game is not only amusing but it also serves to help players learn to identify various knots by sense of touch, a useful accomplishment in the dark.

The only equipment required for two or three contestants is two or three collections of six or eight well-made knots, each one different, tied in 12-inch lengths of sash cord. Identical sets are given each player. The contestants are blindfolded and may stand or sit with a set of knots, placed in a little heap, before each. When the leader of the game calls "Go!" each player picks up the knots one by one, in any order, and whispers the name of each to a non-player, standing directly behind him. This tally keeper, one for each player, quickly notes, on a slip of paper, the name stated; and the contestant puts down the knot, as soon as he has named it, in a separate pile. The tally keeper, who should be a good knot tyer, identifies each knot as it is laid down by his contestant, and marks the knot right or wrong on the slip. As soon as a contestant has identified a knot and laid it down, he picks up another and tries to identify it. This method of play continues until each player has named or tried to name the knots in his heap.

The winner of the contest, of course, is the one fastest and most accurate in naming the knots. However, the leader of the game may decide that a slower player who has named all or most of the knots correctly has won, if the first player to finish has made an error or two in identifying his knots.

This game may also be played by one player at a time naming each knot aloud and working against time, which is kept by the leader or a tally keeper. The player who names the most knots correctly in the shortest time wins.

Various types of knots, but all different, can be used to meet the knot-tying ability of the contestants. The difficulty of the game may be increased by introducing a few trick knots into each set. The thief knot, for instance, and a square knot may be placed in each heap, and a granny too may be added for good measure. Adding the single and the double carrick bend, and other knots of that type, makes the game interesting both for the more seasoned knot tyers and for the audience.

KNOTTY

This game was popular with both children and grown-ups among the Pueblo Indians.

A length of sash cord or light rope, about 18 inches long, is given to each of two or four players; and two contestants compete, one against the other, in this guessing game. The two players sit facing each other about ten feet apart. One player holds the cord behind his back and makes from one to four knots in it, or he may make none, if he prefers. When he has finished making the number of knots he wishes, and is still holding the cord behind his back with his left hand, he brings his right hand out in front of him as a sign that he is ready. His opponent now guesses the number of knots, if any, on the cord. After each guess, the player brings the cord from behind his back with his left hand, so that the other player can see whether his guess was right or wrong.

This game can be played in two ways. Players may take turns guessing, or, if they prefer, one player continues to guess until he guesses wrong, then the other player guesses. Players keep score, and the player with the higher score wins.

The Indians used to try to fool each other, while making knots, by pretending to tie four knots, when they were actually tying only one, or none; at other times, they would race to tie four knots in the time usually taken to tie only one or two. In order to keep the game moving at a good pace, players should not take too long either to tie the knots or to do the guessing.

When four players contest, the two winners then compete against each other.

KNOT RACE

This contest gives the participants a chance to try to tie four easy or not-so-easy knots in a hurry. Contestants always find it difficult to tie knots when competing against time, and the spectators find their efforts entertaining.

The gear required for four players is eight small paper plates, two for each player, and twelve 3-foot lengths of sash cord, three for each player. Three lengths of cord are placed on each of four plates, set 3 feet apart at one end of the room. The other four plates are placed 3 feet apart at the opposite end of the room, 20 to 30 feet away if possible, directly in line with the other plates. One contestant stands behind each of these empty plates, which form the starting end.

When each player is standing upright, behind a plate, the leader of the game calls "Go!" Each player immediately runs to his second plate, directly opposite, picks up *one length* of cord, runs back to the starting plate, ties *any one* of the knots named by the leader, places it *in* the plate, and runs back to the plate for another length of cord.

Each player continues in this way until all three knots have been tied, then raises a hand above his head to show the leader or judge that all three knots have been completed. The leader keeps track of the order of completion by the first, second, and third players who have completed the knots, and checks each knot to be sure that it is correctly tied.

The winner, of course, is the player who is fastest and most accurate in knot tying. However, if the player who finishes second has all three knots correctly tied, and the player who finished first has only two knots correctly tied, the leader may declare the second player the winner or decide that the race was a tie between the two players.

This contest may be made fairly easy by using three easy knots, perhaps the square, bowline, sheepshank, *or* sheet bend, figure-of-eight, and fisherman's knot, each tied with *one piece* of cord. Should the leader wish knots such as the sheet bend and the fisherman's knot tied with *two* cords each, extra lengths of cord must be provided. The contest may be made a little more difficult by using four knots instead of three and, naturally, considerably harder by using more difficult knots.

KNOT PAIRS

This is a guessing game, perhaps even a thought transference game, to some degree. It also promotes the tying of knots, under difficulties, without watching the formation in progress. The only gear required is an 18-inch length of sash cord for each player.

Players pair off and face each other, 4 feet apart. The leader states that they have a choice of tying any one of four basic knots, such as the square knot, figure-of-eight, sheepshank, and bowline, behind the back, with one length of cord.

Each player holds his length of cord behind his back. The leader calls "Go!" and waits a few moments to give the players time to decide on and make the knots which they have chosen. Then he calls "Show!" and each player brings the knot he has made round in front, holding it in one hand. In some cases, it happens with surprising frequency, that the knots are the same. The contestants try again until they both make identical knots twice in succession.

When only two play this game, the point is to see how many times in succession the two players make the same knot. When four or more players participate, the pair which succeeds in duplicating the most knots, in four or six tries, wins. This is where the thought transference comes in.

KNOT SHOW

Another good game, to produce quick knotting under adverse conditions, is the following. The players pair off, each using an 18-inch length of sash cord. The leader crisply names a basic knot, and the two players try to tie it as quickly as possible, behind their backs. Immediately a player finishes the knot, he brings it from behind his back and holds it in front of him. The leader awards first and second place, after verifying that the knots are correctly tied.

TRAVOIS RACE

This amusing and exciting race provides knot tyers the opportunity to demonstrate their skill and speed in knot tying and lashing, while providing fun for the onlookers. The only gear required for each team of two contestants is detailed in Chapter 5 under "Making a Travois." Each team also has a large bundle to tie onto the finished travois and a length of light rope long enough to tie the bundle securely in place on the crosspiece. The bundle should be the same shape and size for each team, and can easily be made of newspaper tied up, before the race, in a piece of cloth or canvas.

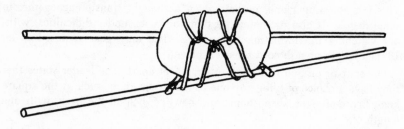

Two long lines are marked on the ground directly opposite each other and about 20 yards apart. One line is used as the start of the race and the gear of each team is placed just behind it, beside the two members of the team, who stand side by side with their heels touching the line, facing the finish line. There should be a space of about 7 feet between teams, decided by the number of teams competing and the space available.

The leader directing the race tells the contestants in advance which hitch—squaw, diamond, or other—must be tied to secure the bundle to the travois crosspiece. On the word "Go!" both contestants on each team start to build the simple travois and lash the bundle onto the crosspiece. Once this is completed, only one contestant pulls the travois to the finish line, while the other runs directly behind the travois in order to retie the bundle if it should fall or drag on the ground. Immediately a bundle touches the ground, the team member in the rear must hold the travois back, calling to the travois puller to stop. The travois must not be moved forward while the bundle is being retied in place, and only when it has been secured can the team race forward again. The first team to reach the finish line with travois and bundle shipshape is the winner.

This race can be made more difficult by having the teams turn at the second line and race back to the starting line, which becomes the winning post, or race around markers set out on a 50-yard run.

Tricky Knot and Rope Stunts

Tricks, teasers, active games that catch players off balance, games that require quickness of thought and movement, and games and stunts that appear to be deceptively easy join company in the following pages. Many of the games will amuse the spectators as much as the contestants, and in some stunts the competitors will ask for second and third chances to do better—only to do worse. It is the uncertainty that makes some games so amusing. Have fun!

MY LADY'S WAIST

This is a very amusing stunt which brings smiles to the faces of rather plump ladies. The only equipment required is a length of smooth rope about 6 feet long and ⅜ inch in diameter.

A few women are needed as volunteers and a few men. To six ladies, there may be twice that number of men, as will be seen. A lady stands in the center of the room and the men are either called in, one by one, from outside the door, or they line up with their faces toward the wall, with the injunction from the judge to "Play fair!"

The test—no easy one—of the first man called is to size up the lady and then use the piece of rope which the judge has given him to form a circle on the floor as close to the exact measurement of the lady's waist as he can estimate. He must then pinch the rope, with thumbs and forefingers, at *exactly* the spot where the two ends crossed. He then places the rope around the lady's waist—still holding the places on the rope where the ends met—to see how close his estimate has been. Nearly always, there is a foot or more to spare, since the men almost invariably allow considerably too much rope. This is a situation which delights the ladies and astonishes the men.

One at a time, the men take turns at estimating the waist measurement of either the same lady or a different one. The man who comes closest to judging the waist size of "his" lady wins.

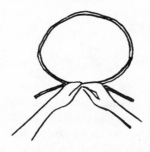

There is no reason why the women should not try their hands at estimating the waist measurements of the men. Probably their results will be about as accurate as the men's estimates of the ladies' waists. Of course, once a number of measurements are guessed, the estimates become more accurate. Nevertheless, it is surprising how far some of the estimates err, even after a few tries.

KOREAN TWIRL

All that is needed to stage this stunt is two or three circles, 3 feet in diameter, each made from thin rope, and some floor space. Played in Korea, this game is popular with players of all ages.

Two or three rope circles are placed, at least 6 feet apart, on the floor or on smooth ground. A volunteer stands in the center of each circle with arms crossed loosely in front, the fingers of the left hand grasping the right ear and the fingers of the right hand holding the left ear.

When the leader calls "Twirl!" each player spins clockwise, in the circle, twirling as quickly as possible but always keeping within the circle. A player who releases his hold on an ear or puts either foot, even a toe, outside the circle is out of the game. Any player who touches the rope with a foot must stop twirling immediately; this is to prevent tripping.

The player who twirls longest and fastest inside his circle is the winner. Players who slow down too much may be ruled out of the game.

Most players find this game considerably more difficult when the leader asks them to twirl counterclockwise.

SKY HIGH!

This is an amusing stunt for the onlookers and will surprise the contestants who perform it for the first time. Since it has never before been published, it will be entirely new to them. The only gear needed for three players is three 3-foot lengths of sash cord, not new, or soft ⅜-inch or ½-inch cotton rope. Three pieces of soft ⅜-inch or ½-inch cotton rope, 7½ inches long, and three pieces of sash cord, not new, 18 inches long, are also required.

The leader of this spoof-stunt lines up the three contestants with 3 feet between players. He then gives each a 3-foot length of sash cord and asks them to hold one end in each hand, so that the cord hangs down to about knee level, more or less, according to the height of the players. He then places one of the three 7½-inch pieces of rope, squeezed to form an inverted V, astride the center of each sash cord.

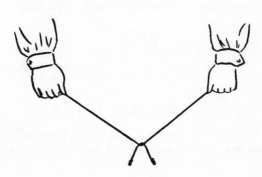

The leader tells the contestants that on the word "Go!" they should jerk their hands and arms apart so that the balanced V's in the center will fly forward and upward, as far as possible. When the word is given, each player does as instructed—with surprisingly little effect. The leader tells the players that perhaps the short length of rope did not give them a fair chance, so he will make up for that. When the sash cords are again allowed to hang down, he places an 18-inch length of cord on the center of each. This longer cord, too, is squeezed into an inverted V, so that the ends hang down. He now expresses the hope that the contestants will do better with these longer, firmer cords. He tells them to be ready for the word "Go!" and in the meantime adds to the spoof by warning anyone near the contestants to get out of the way so that the catapulted cords will have room to fly as far as possible. Then, urging the contestants to propel their cords to a record distance, he calls "Go!"

What happens the second time is also a surprise! The player who projects his two cords the fartherest is the winner.

Willing volunteers will be found to take the places of the former contestants!

KNOT-TO-BE

This is a little stunt which is most puzzling to anyone who has not seen it, but once seen it is always remembered. For this reason, those called on by a leader to tie this knot should be called into the room one at a time.

The stunt may be presented in this way. The leader places a 2- or 3-foot length of rope on a table or on the floor and asks someone who does not know the trick to make a knot in the center of the rope while holding one end of the rope in each hand.

This can be done only by folding the arms before picking up each end of the rope. When the arms are unfolded, the knot forms on the rope automatically.

SQUAT ROPE TUG

The leader of this game chooses two, four, or six players of about the same weight. The players pair off and stand 6 feet apart, facing each other.

Each player is given the knotted end of a 6-foot length of rope. (One length of rope is needed for every two players.)

When the leader calls "Ready!" the two opponents squat on their heels, holding the rope taut between them, but not straining on it. On the word "Go!" each pulls on the rope, trying to unbalance the other. They may pull steadily or by sharp tugs. The winner is the one who manages to upset his opponent most often, on a two-out-of-three-wins basis.

The length of rope may be increased, up to 10 feet. In that case, the two contestants squat 10 feet apart so that there is no slack on the rope.

TOE-TO-HEEL BALANCE

Two players need a 6-foot length of rope to play this game. They stand facing each other, each holding one end of the rope in either hand. Each contestant stands with the toe of one foot touching the heel of the other foot. Once the leader of the game calls "Tug!" the players must not change the positions of their feet in any way. Each player tugs his end of rope in an effort to make his opponent move his feet or lose his balance, thus losing that tug.

Players may hold their arms to one side while tugging or tug with arms raised or lowered, so long as they do not move their feet. The first player to do so, even while trying to throw his opponent off balance, loses that tug. The winner can best be decided on the basis of two out of three tugs.

OCEAN WAVES

For this game, a 16-foot length of rope about ½ inch or more in diameter is required. A solid rubber ball about the size of a tennis ball is put into a small, strong, cloth bag. The mouth of the bag is tied to one end of the rope.

Holding the rope by the end, the leader moves it up and down lightly to form ripples and waves. The weight of the ball, at the other end, keeps that end of the rope close to the ground. Once the rope is in motion and the leader calls "Jump!" the players try to jump back and forth over the rope without being touched on legs or feet by it. If the rope touches a player, or a player the rope, he is out of the game.

By practicing and stooping down, the leader can make the waves rise 18 inches or more from the ground and can quickly make them lower or higher, to catch the players off guard. The game may be played with a longer, heavier rope and may be made more difficult or more simple, to suit the ages of the players. A good man with a rope will not require any weight at its free end.

MAN-REEF-THIEF

This amusing little stunt game is played under different names all over the globe. Young and old play it as Man, Gun, Tiger in Argentina; and, in Great Britain, it is contested as Hunter, Gun, Rabbit. This version, especially devised for knot tyers, uses different symbols from any other version.

No equipment is required for this game, and there can be from two to ten participants, contesting in pairs. They stand in pairs, one player directly opposite the other, about two paces apart. A leader shows them the symbols:

a closed fist for the *man*,
a raised finger for the *reef knot*,
and a clutching hand, fingers outward, for the *thief knot*.

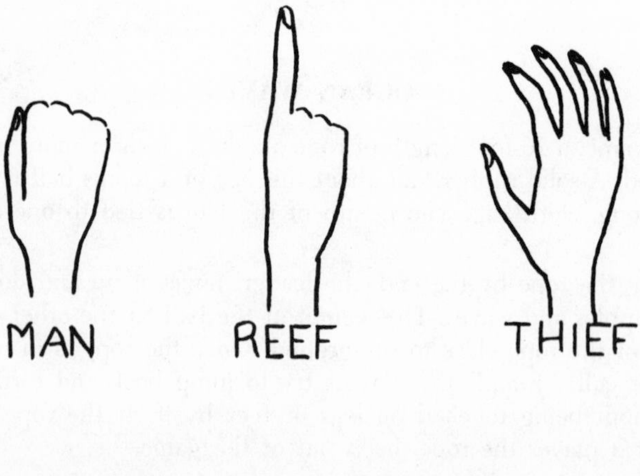

MAN   REEF   THIEF

All three symbols are made with the right hand. The scoring is simple, and the winner is decided as follows:

The *man* devised the *reef knot* and wins over the reef knot,
The *reef knot*, more useful than the *thief knot*, wins over the thief knot,
The *thief knot* fools the *man* and wins over the man.

To begin the first series of three tries, the players turn their backs to each other. A leader or one of the contestants calls "Ready" slowly, so that each player has time to think and get his hand symbol ready. Then, on the word "Go!" both players in each pair swing completely around to face each other, with the hand making the symbol held out at about waist level. Should both players make the same sign—and this happens fairly frequently—that try is considered a tie and neither scores.

The players in each pair, instead of turning around to make the symbol each time, may face each other, about one pace apart, with their hands behind their backs. The sign is made behind the back and the hand brought forward on the word "Go!"

TETHERED! *

The Indians of the Northwest Coast and the Eskimos played this amusing and strenuous game. Perhaps the credit for devising the game should go to the Eskimos who are a merry, game-loving people, especially fond of the man-to-man-challenge type of games. A clean floor, old clothes, or a patch of smooth, grassy ground, each can have a place in this challenge game. The only gear required is a piece of soft rope, about ¾ inch in diameter and 30 inches long, for each two contestants. Thinner rope may be used if a strip of strong, thick cloth about 2 inches wide, or a folded newspaper, is wrapped around the ankles of the challengers first, when they are in position, before their ankles are tied together.

This is how the foot-pull game was played by the Indians and the Eskimos. Two players of about equal weight went down on hands and knees, facing away from each other, with their right ankles side by side. Their right ankles were then fastened together with a loop which covered their ankles.

On the shout "Pull!" each contestant tried to drag the other backward a few paces, to decide the winner. This contest is best decided on a two-wins-out-of-three basis. Sometimes four or five pairs of contestants com-

---

* From *Treasury of Memory-Making Campfires*, by Allan A. Macfarlan (New York: Association Press, 1963).

peted at the same time, the champion being chosen by matching the winners of each pair of challengers, until the three final pulls decided the champion.

As in all such games, leaders devised variations, such as pulling with the left foot, and *both* feet, which considerably increased the difficulty for the challengers and added to the amusement of the spectators.

TRICK-BALANCE TUG

This is an amusing contest in which players of approximately the same weight are matched. The only gear required is a 15-foot length of stout rope, about ½ inch in diameter, and two paper plates, about 6 inches in diameter, for each pair of contestants. (One, two, or three pairs of contestants can compete at once, but one pair at a time causes better concentration of the onlookers' attention.) The rope should be marked 3 feet from each end with indelible ink or pencil or by a piece of colored twine securely tied around it.

The contestants squat directly opposite each other and 9 feet apart. The leader gives each contestant one end of the rope and puts a paper plate as a marker beside each, to assure their remaining the correct distance apart, 9 feet. Each must remain beside his marker throughout the contest. This gives each player 3 feet of spare rope, and this "surplus" rope is what the contestants use to try to trick each other.

When the opponents squat in their ready-to-pull position, at the start of the contest, they hold the rope with one hand just in front of the 3-foot mark and the other hand somewhere behind it. When the leader calls "Ready!" each player takes the strain lightly so that the rope is held taut between them. On the command "Pull!" they tighten up on the rope, each trying to throw the other off balance so that he is forced to fall backward or place a hand on the ground for support. A player can accomplish this by tugging hard, then suddenly and unexpectedly releasing a foot or two of rope. A little practice helps to develop this strategy. The player who is thrown off balance so that he falls backward or who has to put a hand on the ground for support loses the match. It is best to decide this contest on a two-wins-out-of-three basis. Invariably, the clever use of the spare rope decides the winner.

ORANGE TUG

Two to six players stand about 3 feet apart on a starting line, marked on the ground or floor, facing a *round* orange which is placed just behind the line by the person directing the game. There is an orange for each player. Directly behind the players, 30 feet away, the finish line is plainly marked on the floor.

Each player is given a 4-foot length of sash cord with a knot tied on

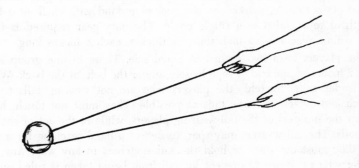

each end. The player holds the cord by the knots, one knot between the fingers of each hand, and places the center of the cord on the ground directly behind the orange.

When the leader calls "Go!" each player tugs the orange toward him with the cord as he walks backward, as quickly as possible, toward the finish line. He continues to do so until his orange has crossed the finish line. The player whose orange crosses first wins.

This contest, despite the fact that it appears easy, requires some skill and patience. Quite often, impatient players are still tugging at their oranges close to the starting point while others are crossing the finish line. Sharp jerks on the cord usually cause the orange to jump over it, while gentler methods make the orange follow along steadily to the winning line.

Variation

This game may be played by teams, with four or six players on each team. One half of the players on each team stand one behind the other at one line while the other half of each team forms behind the other line, and directly opposite. As soon as the first player from the starting line reaches the second line, the first player at that line races the orange back again and the race continues, in this relay style, until the last player on each team has crossed the finish line. The team to finish first is the winner.

SNATCH!

This is a game for ten to eighteen fast-moving players, who play within a 20- or 30-foot circle, marked on the floor or ground with chalk or a long length of rope coiled in a single circle. The only gear required is from five to nine pieces of ½-inch rope, or thicker, each 8 inches long.

The players form two groups of equal size. Those in one group each tuck 2 inches of one end of rope loosely, under the belt, at the back. When the leader calls "Snatch!" the players who are not wearing tails try to snatch and detach as many tails as possible. They must not touch, hold, or bar the progress of the tail-wearing players, while in the act of snatching tails. The tail wearers may spar, to deflect a hand reaching for a tail, but they must not push or hold the tail snatchers in any way. Any tail bearer who sits down to prevent his tail from being taken is ruled out of the game and his tail is forfeit to the would-be snatcher who was thwarted in his snatch.

When all tails have been taken, the players change places, in order to give the former tail bearers a chance to get even.

This game can be played with as few as three players, one wearing the tail and two trying to get possession of it. The leader should be on the alert to see that the play never becomes rough and should rule out of the game any players who play too strenuously.

HOLD FAST!

This is a game of opposites, played with a 30- or 40-foot length of ½-inch rope, joined at the ends with a sheet bend. Twenty or more players can play at the same time, or the game can be played with the same length of rope by only six or ten players.

The players sit in a circle on the floor or ground, each holding onto the rope so that it forms a circle. The rope is held above waist level by one hand, either right or left, with the knuckles upward.

A leader stands in the center of the circle, or just outside, and calls "Hold fast!" or "Let go!" at frequent intervals. The difficulty for the players lies in the fact that they must do exactly the *opposite* of the order given. When the leader calls "Hold fast!" each player must instantly let go and those who do not are ruled out of the game. When "Let go!" is called, each hand holds on, and any player who even temporarily lets go his hold on the rope is out of the game.

The leader uses psychology to cause as many players as possible to do the wrong thing. He may give the same order twice running, then change to the other command. He may call in a soft voice, changing to a loud and commanding voice, or adopting an urgent tone, from time to time.

There are always a few players who cannot be caught and, after a few final commands, they are considered tied for winning place.

GROMMET GRAB

This is an adaptation of a game played in Japan, by both children and grown-ups, which requires three players with quick reflexes.

The only equipment for this stunt game is a length of rather stiff rope, 6 feet 9 inches long and ⅜ to ½ inch in diameter, and a rope grommet 3 or 4 inches in diameter. Two players squat or kneel, one holding each end of the rope, which has one loose, single knot in the center and is opened into a loop about 6 inches in diameter. A third player kneels on the floor exactly opposite the loop and about 12 inches away from it, on either side.

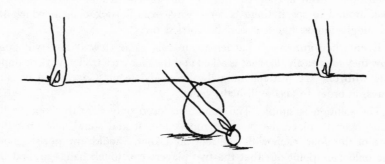

A leader places the grommet on the opposite side of the loop from the player and 5 or 6 inches away from it. The game is now ready to flash into action, as soon as the two players holding the rope keep it open in a round loop, with the lower edge just touching the floor. It takes a little practice on the part of these players to keep a nice round loop, just touching the floor for support. As soon as they are ready, the leader says "Begin!" and, shortly after, the kneeling player makes a swift grab for the grommet, trying to grasp it and take it back to his side of the rope before the two rope holders can pull the noose tight and trap his hand or wrist. This takes cooperation and split-second timing on the part of the two rope holders, since the hand must be taken prisoner.

The grommet snatcher is allowed 2 points each time he succeeds in snatching the grommet, and the rope handlers lose 2 points each time they tighten the noose without catching the hand or wrist. Just being touched by the rope does not count against the grommet grabber, who is permitted to feint only once in each of the four tries he is allowed. The rope pullers lose one point each time they tighten the rope needlessly, when they only imagine that the grabber is going to grab. The game may be decided on a 6-point basis, or even more, should the leader find that the nervous rope pullers are throwing away points needlessly.

UNTOUCHABLE!

The only gear required for this game is a piece of small rope 18 inches long, with a knot tied on each end. The players are shown the rope, and the game leader asks for two volunteers who believe that they can stand each with one foot on a knot, in such a position that they cannot touch each other, even if they try hard to do so. The leader advises them to look around to see if there is some way, even a trick one, in which the seemingly impossible feat can be carried out.

Even when grown-ups participate in this game, few if any will guess how they may easily do what is asked and they may try tricky ways of standing, with one toe just touching the knot, and leaning backward or sideways, in order to accomplish the feat.

The solution is simple. The volunteers need only take the rope to the door, open it, place the piece of rope under it and stand, one on either side of the door, each with one foot on a knot. Should any purist among the onlookers point out that the two players can touch hands around the open side of the door, the door may be closed and the stunt still carried out.

The leader should bar anyone in the group who *knows* how the stunt is performed, and, in order to give more volunteers the fun of trying, all players except the two who are using the rope may be asked to face the wall and be put on their honor not to look. In a small group, another way to let more players try is to have three or more rope lengths ready and let six or more players figure out the solution at the same time.

WEB WEAVING*

The real fun in this American Indian game, also known as Cat's Cradle, is experimentation. Sometimes interesting and pretty patterns appear unexpectedly. The string pattern which follows is one of the least difficult ones, since it is formed by two partners working together. The diagrams illustrate this form of the game. The three fingers which do the work are indicated as follows in the drawings:

1–the thumb
2–the index finger
5–the little finger
(3–the middle finger, used only in the opening position)

For beginners and average players, strong, medium-weight twine in about 68-inch lengths is suitable for most designs and provides a little leeway in handling certain patterns. The two ends of the cord may be joined with the reef knot, but real experts would not dream of *tying* the two ends together—they splice or weave them together! Strings must be kept taut to assure an even pattern on both sides.

The barred diamond is an easy partner pattern. It is woven in this way. In opening A, one player puts both hands up through the oblong of string, making a single loop around each hand. The string passes around the index finger, across the back of each hand, as illustrated on the next page.

---

* From *Book of American Indian Games*, by Allan A. Macfarlan (New York: Association Press, 1958).

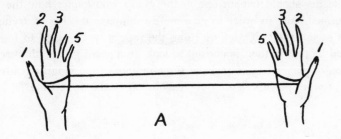

A

Now, pass the middle finger of the right hand up through the loop at the palm of the left hand. With the middle finger of the left hand, pick up the loop at the palm of the right hand, in the same way. You now have the opening or starting position, shown in Figure B.

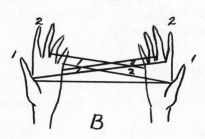

B

Your partner joins the game at this point and puts thumb and index finger of each hand down through the crossed strings on each side, as indicated by numbers 1 and 2 in Figure B. The thumb and index finger are brought together at the tips so that the string cannot escape. Then, they come across the two outside strings, around and underneath, coming up through the center. The hands are now pulled apart to make the string taut, and the thumb and forefinger opened out, making the pattern shown in Figure C.

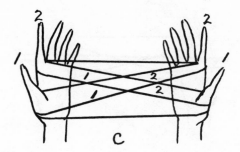

Pass the thumb and index finger of each hand down through the crossed strings and bring them across, around and under the outside strings, bringing the hands up through the center. Pull the strings taut, and you have Figure D.

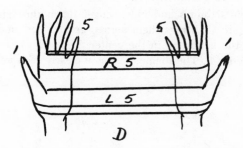

Your partner now takes the center string on the right side with the little finger of the left hand, pulls it a little to the left, then reaches through the arch thus formed and takes the center string on the left with the little finger of the right hand and pulls it a little to the right. In this way, the strings are now crossed. Your partner must be careful to hold each string

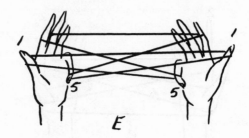

tightly with the little fingers so that it cannot escape. Now the thumbs and index fingers are brought across the outside strings, around and under, coming up in the center, as before. The strings are pulled taut, resulting in Figure E.

The strings are already crossed; so all you have to do is pass the thumb and index finger through the crossed strings on each side and bring the hands out, around, over, and *down* through the outer strings. This movement is the opposite of the usual way in which the hands are brought *up* through the outer strings. Now you have what appears to be Figure C again. Actually it is a little different, because it, in turn, leads to Figure F which is quite different from the others.

Your partner puts thumb and index finger down through the crossed strings, as in Figure C, brings them across, around and under the outer strings, bringing the hands up in the center. The strings are pulled taut, and you have Figure F. The diamond is now clearly seen and it has now only to be barred.

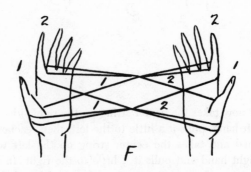

You now put the thumb and index finger down through the crossed strings and bring the hands up through the center. When the strings are pulled taut, Figure G makes its appearance, the barred diamond, and the figure is complete.

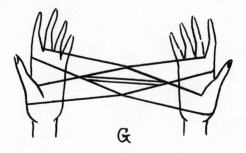

G

Modern Knot Mystery and Magic

The average magician, who knows a lot about "magic" knots and very little about real knots, often finds an intimate audience of knot tyers too perceptive for his comfort. Exhibiting a bowline, tied in a flourish with one hand, he discovers that his audience is aware that it is a fake knot and not a real bowline. Because of this audience perception in knot identification, only a few "spoof" knots are included in this chapter.

A successful knot and rope magician must work accurately, smoothly, casually, and confidently. Anyone who has taught knot tying knows that the method of tying even a simple, new knot is hard enough to follow and that conjurers' knots present even greater difficulties. A number of the tricks given here were performed by North American Indian tribal "merry-makers," and their counterparts, the tricksters of the Guianas, and were known to conjurers in Europe prior to the fifteenth century.

The best rope for most rope magic is soft, hollow-center (without core), braided, cotton clothesline. Should a less pliant rope be required for some stunt in these pages, the fact is noted. The few easy-to-perform tricks given here are for the amateur magician and, as fitting in a book devoted to ropes and knots, practically no paraphernalia of any kind, apart from rope, cord, or string, is required. This makes things much easier for the performer, since there are no gadgets to palm, conceal, manipulate—or drop on the floor, at the wrong moment.

No "magic" rope ties and releases are included in the tricks and stunts which follow, since the audiences of today, even a small private audience watching an amateur display of rope and knot magic, are not naïve and gullible, and many people among them know how to tie real knots! In the past, the Davenport Brothers were "spiritualist" fakers who fooled committees from the audience. These committees knew little or nothing about knots, ropes, or ties, and absolutely nothing about certain apparently natural positions in which wrists, arms, legs, and bodies could be placed to make anything resembling secure binding impossible. The psychology of these tricksters—pained expressions, little gasps of feigned pain, to prevent the ties being made tight, and subtle suggestions, by movements, of how they could be securely bound in the positions in which they sat or stood—completely fooled the committee from the audience. Actually, the members of the committees merely bound these fakers in the way in which they wished to be tied. A few well-tied knots and hitches, such as the clove hitch, the highwayman's hitch, and other subtle ties which would tighten under strain, would have completely immobilized these mystifiers for a week!

In a book in which perhaps some mention of the East Indian rope trick should be made, it need only be said that after considerable firsthand research, the authors firmly believe that in reality, the "feat" never has been and never will be actually performed. Invariably, the effect has been achieved by suggestion and hallucination, including mass hypnotism. When compared with the rope trick of the East Indian fakirs, the feat of Jack, of Beanstalk fame, is vibrant with possibility.

The "feats" detailed in this chapter are given in a sequence ranging from very easy to a little more difficult though, with a little practice, none of them is actually difficult. A few of the tricks are fairly well known but worth setting down for the many who may not know them, while others are little known and well worthwhile.

CORD-MATES

This is the old handcuff trick, practiced by conjurers all over the globe, under a new name. It will, without fail, puzzle and frustrate members of the most sophisticated audience who do not know the solution to this escape problem. The cord-mates are not supposed to remove the cords from their wrists and one of the most side-splitting parts of the performance comes when, after a few futile efforts to escape, one of the pair takes charge and tells the other a sure method of release. This consists of stepping over the bights of the cords, bringing them over their heads and similar antics, which are most amusing to watch. Not to be outdone, the second member of the pair takes over and the gyrations usually become more strenuous than ever, with the same unsatisfactory result—both are still prisoners!

Before selecting a few pairs of boys and girls, to form mixed couples, the conjurer, or leader, assures the performers that the stunt can be done, *without* removing the cords from the wrists. He then puts the participants on their honor not to slip even one wrist free of the cord while trying to regain freedom.

How It Is Done. Use a 4-foot length of sash cord; tie a stopper knot at each end, then form a running loop at each end by tying a slip knot in each. Two of these are needed for each pair of cord-mates.

Ask for two volunteers from the audience. For convenience we shall call them A and B. Slip a loop over each of A's wrists, then over one of B's wrists. Now, bring the cord up and over A's cord, as it hangs down, and slip the loop over B's other wrist, so that the cords cross as in the diagram. Tell A and B that they should try to escape without removing any loop.

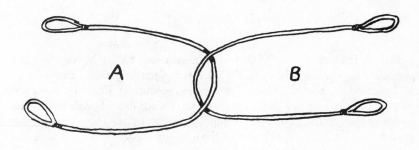

Let them struggle a few minutes, much to the amusement of the audience, and when they agree that they cannot do it, you take over. Take the cord between B's *left* wrist and the bight and slip it *up* through the under side of the loop at A's *right* wrist, then *over* his right hand, and they are free.

This trick can also be done in another way, by taking B's cord and bringing it *over* A's *left* hand, just behind the wrist, pushing it under the wrist loop and pulling the rope gently, over his hand, so that it becomes free of A's cord.

LOOP TRAP

This is an interesting type of finger trap which can catch a finger or not, at the will of the conjurer.

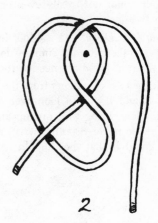

How It Is Done. Lay a 3-foot length of sash cord on a table or other flat surface. Arrange the cord as in Figure 1 and place your finger in the loop, as indicated by the black dot. Ask for two volunteers from the audience to pull the ends of the cord; and, as they do so, one at each end, your finger is free of the cord and cannot be caught by it. Then arrange the cord as in Figure 2 and ask one of them to put his finger in the loop. As you pull the ends of the cord, his finger will be caught.

The secret lies in the way you lay the cord. When the left end is *over* the bight, it will trap the finger but when it is *under* the bight, it cannot.

PRESTO—CHANGE!

Two rings on a cord are covered with a handkerchief and, as two volunteers from the audience each hold an end of the cord, the conjurer makes the rings change places.

How It Is Done. Make a loop and place a brass ring about the center of a 3-foot length of sash cord, then tie a square knot nearly halfway between the bight and the ends of the cord. Place a black ring of the same size on the cord and make a second square knot about halfway between the first knot and the cord ends. (The conjurer should be able to identify the rings by touch.)

Ask for two volunteers to hold the ends of the cord, one at each end. Cover the cord and rings completely with a handkerchief and tell the audience that you are going to make the rings change places. With the handkerchief covering your movements, loosen the center knot and work the brass ring *up* along one side of the cord, through the knot, and into the top loop. Then work the black ring *down* along the opposite side of the cord, through the knot and down into the lower loop. With some practice, this can be done in just a few seconds. Be sure to tighten the square knot again before removing the handkerchief.

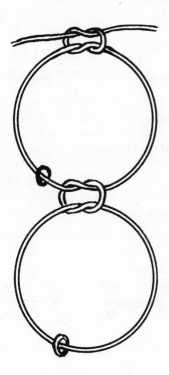

RING ON A STRING

This is a simple but effective trick. The magician places cord loops over his wrists, then holds up a ring for the audience to see. He may invite them to inspect both the wrist ties and the ring. He then assures the audience that he will tie the ring onto the cord without removing either loop from his wrists.

How It Is Done. To save time, have a 3-foot length of cord already prepared with a wrist loop, tied with a slip knot, at each end. Slip a loop over each wrist but leave about ½ inch leeway at each wrist. Turn your back on the audience a moment and quickly make a bight in the center of the cord and pass it away from you, through the small metal ring. Now pass the bight *over* the right hand so that it comes behind the wrist loop, away from the hand. Then pass the bight *under* the wrist loop and back over the right hand. Face the audience, and the ring will now be fastened on the string.

It is apparent to the audience that the cord will have to be removed from one wrist or both, to remove the ring.

UNDERHAND OVERHAND

The onlookers will see three knots disappear at the jerk of a rope.

How It Is Done. Make three overhand knots, several inches apart, in a 6-foot length of rope. Leave them loose enough to pass the fingers through easily. From the *front* of the knot pass the fingers of the right hand through each knot, starting at the right-hand side, then take the rope end at the left-hand side between the thumb and index finger of the right hand. Jerk the rope forward and the knots will disappear as though by magic.

This can also be done with more knots, if desired.

KNOTS TO NAUGHT

This is a simple knot trick which will puzzle the audience. The knots in both Figure 1 and Figure 2 should be practiced until they can be tied quickly and correctly.

How It Is Done. Use a 4-foot length of rope about ⅜ inch in diameter. Tie the overhand knot shown in Figure 1, leaving about two thirds of the length of rope to work with at side A. Then tie another overhand knot above it, as in Figure 2. Note that in Figure 2 the overhand knots are *not* the same, the upper bight passing *over* the lower one and end B, on the left side, and *under* the lower one and end A, at the right. This is *important.* Next, pass end A *down* through the lower loop and up *over* the lower knot, but *under* the second knot, as in Figure 3.

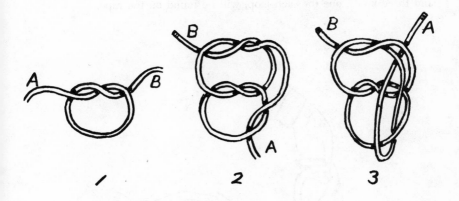

At this point, the knot looks hopeless, and this should be pointed out to the audience. Then, holding end A in the right hand and end B in the left, pull the hands apart, making the knots disappear.

If you prefer, drop end B, while keeping end A in the right hand, and jerk the rope to make the knots vanish.

This knot may also be made on a flat surface and covered with a handkerchief. Two volunteers may be recruited from the audience. When one pulls at each end of the rope, the handkerchief is removed and the knots have vanished.

KNOTS FROM THE AIR

To the audience, the effect of this trick is that the rope is casually coiled in the right hand, and that when it is jerked forward, with one end still held in the right hand, three overhand knots seem to have formed in the air.

How It Is Done. Actually, the knots are formed because of the way in which the rope is coiled; perhaps *looped* is a better term.

A 6-foot length of ⅜- or ½-inch-in-diameter soft, cotton rope is required for this trick. Hold one end of the rope in the right hand and, with the left hand, make an overhand loop and place it loosely over the fingertips of the right hand. Repeat this twice more, each loop being placed in front of the other, so that you have three loops. Then, pass the left end of the rope unobtrusively through the loops and grasp it firmly with the thumb and index finger of the right hand. Now, throw the rope forward with a jerk; and three knots, one for each loop, will be found on the rope.

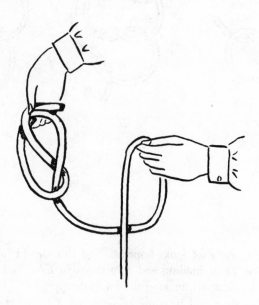

It is most unlikely that anyone in the audience will note how the loops are being formed, but unless the end is passed through the loops smoothly and naturally, someone may notice this move. Even if someone does, he will most likely be unable to duplicate the magic knots.

Some conjurers talk to the audience, as a cover-up, throughout this trick.

THE DISAPPEARING KNOTS

If the magician wishes, he may make the knots in the Knots From the Air trick disappear, as though by magic.

How It Is Done. Slip the fingers of the left hand through the loop knots, starting with the left-hand side and ending with the right-hand knot. Slip the fingers through the knot at the left-hand end, from the *front*, then the second, from the front, and the third also. Grasp the right-hand end of the rope between the thumb and index finger of the left hand, and the left end of the rope by the thumb and index finger of the right hand. Jerk the hands apart, keeping the hold on the ends of the rope, and the knots will mysteriously disappear.

If you prefer, you may let the left-hand side of the rope hang loose, while firmly holding the right-hand end of the rope in the left hand, and jerk the rope forward to make the knots disappear.

FINGER WEAVING

This mystifying string trick invariably surprises the audience, who find it difficult or impossible to duplicate.

How It Is Done. Knot a 3-foot length of medium-weight string to form a loop and lace it through the left fingers and around the thumb, as illustrated.

Holding the left hand palm up, loop one end of the string around the little finger, crossing the front string *over* the back one. As they are woven between the other fingers, be sure always to cross the front string *over* the back ones. Note how the strings are arranged at the arrow in the diagram because if the strings cross each other at the thumb, the trick will not work. After the string has been properly laced on the third finger, bring it *down* around the thumb and back *up* to the third finger, while the other string goes around the tip of the thumb, behind the index finger, and the lacing starts again, in the same way as before, at the third finger.

After lacing the string around the little finger, slip both loops from the thumb and pull the remaining string at the little finger with the right hand. It will pull free of your fingers, appearing to go right through them.

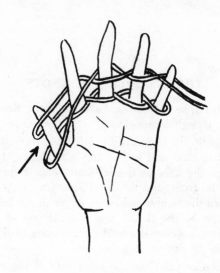

KNOT THERE

When a loop and knot disappear from a piece of string, the audience has reason to be puzzled. This is one of a number of string tricks which deceive the eye.

How It Is Done. Make an overhand knot in the center of a 3-foot length of sash cord or medium-weight string, then a double overhand at the end, as shown in the diagram. Ask someone to remove the knot without untying the ends. When he gives up, turn your back to the audience or place a handkerchief over the cord and your hands. Push the center knot up to become part of the end knot. Pull the cord taut.

INDEX

Index

A CATALOGUE OF SELECTED DOVER BOOKS
IN ALL FIELDS OF INTEREST

A CATALOGUE OF SELECTED DOVER
BOOKS IN ALL FIELDS OF INTEREST

RACKHAM'S COLOR ILLUSTRATIONS FOR WAGNER'S RING. Rackham's finest mature work—all 64 full-color watercolors in a faithful and lush interpretation of the *Ring*. Full-sized plates on coated stock of the paintings used by opera companies for authentic staging of Wagner. Captions aid in following complete Ring cycle. Introduction. 64 illustrations plus vignettes. 72pp. 8⅝ x 11¼. 23779-6 Pa. $6.00

CONTEMPORARY POLISH POSTERS IN FULL COLOR, edited by Joseph Czestochowski. 46 full-color examples of brilliant school of Polish graphic design, selected from world's first museum (near Warsaw) dedicated to poster art. Posters on circuses, films, plays, concerts all show cosmopolitan influences, free imagination. Introduction. 48pp. 9⅜ x 12¼. 23780-X Pa. $6.00

GRAPHIC WORKS OF EDVARD MUNCH, Edvard Munch. 90 haunting, evocative prints by first major Expressionist artist and one of the greatest graphic artists of his time: *The Scream, Anxiety, Death Chamber, The Kiss, Madonna,* etc. Introduction by Alfred Werner. 90pp. 9 x 12. 23765-6 Pa. $5.00

THE GOLDEN AGE OF THE POSTER, Hayward and Blanche Cirker. 70 extraordinary posters in full colors, from Maitres de l'Affiche, Mucha, Lautrec, Bradley, Cheret, Beardsley, many others. Total of 78pp. 9⅜ x 12¼. 22753-7 Pa. $5.95

THE NOTEBOOKS OF LEONARDO DA VINCI, edited by J. P. Richter. Extracts from manuscripts reveal great genius; on painting, sculpture, anatomy, sciences, geography, etc. Both Italian and English. 186 ms. pages reproduced, plus 500 additional drawings, including studies for *Last Supper,* Sforza monument, etc. 860pp. 7⅞ x 10¾. (Available in U.S. only) 22572-0, 22573-9 Pa., Two-vol. set $15.90

THE CODEX NUTTALL, as first edited by Zelia Nuttall. Only inexpensive edition, in full color, of a pre-Columbian Mexican (Mixtec) book. 88 color plates show kings, gods, heroes, temples, sacrifices. New explanatory, historical introduction by Arthur G. Miller. 96pp. 11⅜ x 8½. (Available in U.S. only) 23168-2 Pa. $7.95

UNE SEMAINE DE BONTÉ, A SURREALISTIC NOVEL IN COLLAGE, Max Ernst. Masterpiece created out of 19th-century periodical illustrations, explores worlds of terror and surprise. Some consider this Ernst's greatest work. 208pp. 8⅛ x 11. 23252-2 Pa. $6.00

DRAWINGS OF WILLIAM BLAKE, William Blake. 92 plates from Book of Job, *Divine Comedy, Paradise Lost*, visionary heads, mythological figures, Laocoon, etc. Selection, introduction, commentary by Sir Geoffrey Keynes. 178pp. 8⅛ x 11. 22303-5 Pa. $4.00

ENGRAVINGS OF HOGARTH, William Hogarth. 101 of Hogarth's greatest works: *Rake's Progress, Harlot's Progress, Illustrations for Hudibras, Before and After, Beer Street and Gin Lane,* many more. Full commentary. 256pp. 11 x 13¾. 22479-1 Pa. $12.95

DAUMIER: 120 GREAT LITHOGRAPHS, Honore Daumier. Wide-ranging collection of lithographs by the greatest caricaturist of the 19th century. Concentrates on eternally popular series on lawyers, on married life, on liberated women, etc. Selection, introduction, and notes on plates by Charles F. Ramus. Total of 158pp. 9⅜ x 12¼. 23512-2 Pa. $6.00

DRAWINGS OF MUCHA, Alphonse Maria Mucha. Work reveals draftsman of highest caliber: studies for famous posters and paintings, renderings for book illustrations and ads, etc. 70 works, 9 in color; including 6 items not drawings. Introduction. List of illustrations. 72pp. 9⅜ x 12¼. (Available in U.S. only) 23672-2 Pa. $4.00

GIOVANNI BATTISTA PIRANESI: DRAWINGS IN THE PIERPONT MORGAN LIBRARY, Giovanni Battista Piranesi. For first time ever all of Morgan Library's collection, world's largest. 167 illustrations of rare Piranesi drawings—archeological, architectural, decorative and visionary. Essay, detailed list of drawings, chronology, captions. Edited by Felice Stampfle. 144pp. 9⅜ x 12¼. 23714-1 Pa. $7.50

NEW YORK ETCHINGS (1905-1949), John Sloan. All of important American artist's N.Y. life etchings. 67 works include some of his best art; also lively historical record—Greenwich Village, tenement scenes. Edited by Sloan's widow. Introduction and captions. 79pp. 8⅜ x 11¼. 23651-X Pa. $4.00

CHINESE PAINTING AND CALLIGRAPHY: A PICTORIAL SURVEY, Wan-go Weng. 69 fine examples from John M. Crawford's matchless private collection: landscapes, birds, flowers, human figures, etc., plus calligraphy. Every basic form included: hanging scrolls, handscrolls, album leaves, fans, etc. 109 illustrations. Introduction. Captions. 192pp. 8⅞ x 11¾. 23707-9 Pa. $7.95

DRAWINGS OF REMBRANDT, edited by Seymour Slive. Updated Lippmann, Hofstede de Groot edition, with definitive scholarly apparatus. All portraits, biblical sketches, landscapes, nudes, Oriental figures, classical studies, together with selection of work by followers. 550 illustrations. Total of 630pp. 9⅛ x 12¼. 21485-0, 21486-9 Pa., Two-vol. set $15.00

THE DISASTERS OF WAR, Francisco Goya. 83 etchings record horrors of Napoleonic wars in Spain and war in general. Reprint of 1st edition, plus 3 additional plates. Introduction by Philip Hofer. 97pp. 9⅜ x 8¼. 21872-4 Pa. $4.00

THE COMPLETE BOOK OF DOLL MAKING AND COLLECTING, Catherine Christopher. Instructions, patterns for dozens of dolls, from rag doll on up to elaborate, historically accurate figures. Mould faces, sew clothing, make doll houses, etc. Also collecting information. Many illustrations. 288pp. 6 x 9. 22066-4 Pa. $4.50

THE DAGUERREOTYPE IN AMERICA, Beaumont Newhall. Wonderful portraits, 1850's townscapes, landscapes; full text plus 104 photographs. The basic book. Enlarged 1976 edition. 272pp. 8¼ x 11¼. 23322-7 Pa. $7.95

CRAFTSMAN HOMES, Gustav Stickley. 296 architectural drawings, floor plans, and photographs illustrate 40 different kinds of "Mission-style" homes from *The Craftsman* (1901-16), voice of American style of simplicity and organic harmony. Thorough coverage of Craftsman idea in text and picture, now collector's item. 224pp. 8⅛ x 11. 23791-5 Pa. $6.00

PEWTER-WORKING: INSTRUCTIONS AND PROJECTS, Burl N. Osborn. & Gordon O. Wilber. Introduction to pewter-working for amateur craftsman. History and characteristics of pewter; tools, materials, step-by-step instructions. Photos, line drawings, diagrams. Total of 160pp. 7⅞ x 10¾. 23786-9 Pa. $3.50

THE GREAT CHICAGO FIRE, edited by David Lowe. 10 dramatic, eyewitness accounts of the 1871 disaster, including one of the aftermath and rebuilding, plus 70 contemporary photographs and illustrations of the ruins—courthouse, Palmer House, Great Central Depot, etc. Introduction by David Lowe. 87pp. 8¼ x 11. 23771-0 Pa. $4.00

SILHOUETTES: A PICTORIAL ARCHIVE OF VARIED ILLUSTRATIONS, edited by Carol Belanger Grafton. Over 600 silhouettes from the 18th to 20th centuries include profiles and full figures of men and women, children, birds and animals, groups and scenes, nature, ships, an alphabet. Dozens of uses for commercial artists and craftspeople. 144pp. 8⅜ x 11¼. 23781-8 Pa. $4.50

ANIMALS: 1,419 COPYRIGHT-FREE ILLUSTRATIONS OF MAMMALS, BIRDS, FISH, INSECTS, ETC., edited by Jim Harter. Clear wood engravings present, in extremely lifelike poses, over 1,000 species of animals. One of the most extensive copyright-free pictorial sourcebooks of its kind. Captions. Index. 284pp. 9 x 12. 23766-4 Pa. $8.95

INDIAN DESIGNS FROM ANCIENT ECUADOR, Frederick W. Shaffer. 282 original designs by pre-Columbian Indians of Ecuador (500-1500 A.D.). Designs include people, mammals, birds, reptiles, fish, plants, heads, geometric designs. Use as is or alter for advertising, textiles, leathercraft, etc. Introduction. 95pp. 8¾ x 11¼. 23764-8 Pa. $3.50

SZIGETI ON THE VIOLIN, Joseph Szigeti. Genial, loosely structured tour by premier violinist, featuring a pleasant mixture of reminiscenes, insights into great music and musicians, innumerable tips for practicing violinists. 385 musical passages. 256pp. 5⅝ x 8¼. 23763-X Pa. $4.00

AMERICAN ANTIQUE FURNITURE, Edgar G. Miller, Jr. The basic coverage of all American furniture before 1840: chapters per item chronologically cover all types of furniture, with more than 2100 photos. Total of 1106pp. 7⅞ x 10¾.   21599-7, 21600-4 Pa., Two-vol. set $17.90

ILLUSTRATED GUIDE TO SHAKER FURNITURE, Robert Meader. Director, Shaker Museum, Old Chatham, presents up-to-date coverage of all furniture and appurtenances, with much on local styles not available elsewhere. 235 photos. 146pp. 9 x 12.   22819-3 Pa. $6.00

ORIENTAL RUGS, ANTIQUE AND MODERN, Walter A. Hawley. Persia, Turkey, Caucasus, Central Asia, China, other traditions. Best general survey of all aspects: styles and periods, manufacture, uses, symbols and their interpretation, and identification. 96 illustrations, 11 in color. 320pp. 6⅛ x 9¼.   22366-3 Pa. $6.95

CHINESE POTTERY AND PORCELAIN, R. L. Hobson. Detailed descriptions and analyses by former Keeper of the Department of Oriental Antiquities and Ethnography at the British Museum. Covers hundreds of pieces from primitive times to 1915. Still the standard text for most periods. 136 plates, 40 in full color. Total of 750pp. 5⅜ x 8½.
23253-0 Pa. $10.00

THE WARES OF THE MING DYNASTY, R. L. Hobson. Foremost scholar examines and illustrates many varieties of Ming (1368-1644). Famous blue and white, polychrome, lesser-known styles and shapes. 117 illustrations, 9 full color, of outstanding pieces. Total of 263pp. 6⅛ x 9¼. (Available in U.S. only)   23652-8 Pa. $6.00